The
SEAWEED
Cookbook

CAROLINE WARWICK-EVANS
and TIM VAN BERKEL

The
SEAWEED
Cookbook

**A guide to edible seaweeds and how
to cook with them**

PHOTOGRAPHY BY DAVID GRIFFEN

LORENZ BOOKS

CONTENTS

SEAWEED, AN INTRODUCTION

Many of us have childhood memories of sliding around on slippery seaweed-coated rocks firmly gripping a bucket and net, pushing aside the vast mats of algae that were blocking our view of the crabs, starfish and guppy trophies we sought (and always returned safely after having compared claw sizes and occasional war wounds received in the chase!), and we are no different. What's more, if someone had told us then that one day we would be eating the seaweed, we too would have probably laughed and thrown some at that person.

In the British Isles alone there are somewhere in the region of 630 different species of seaweed. The most obvious of these are the dark-brown types found washed up along the shoreline, which are a regular feature of a trip to the seaside. But investigate just a little further and you'll be led down through the bright-green pools of sea lettuce and then on into the deep and mysterious kelp forests that conceal thick clumps of dulse and a wealth of marine life. All of these can be used as ingredients in a huge variety of dishes and are now making their way into mainstream cooking. Treated as a vegetable, flaked and sprinkled as a seasoning condiment, used as a replacement for salt, munched as a snack, or rehydrated and eaten raw, seaweeds offer a diverse and highly nutritious component to all kinds of meals, snacks or drinks.

From an environmental point of view, eating seaweed is a winner. It grows without human help, absorbing minerals and other nutrients from the sea around it. There is ample space in which it can be cultivated if necessary, and its production does not need to impact the environment in a negative way if done sensibly. In fact, seaweed cultivation may prove environmentally beneficial since it can also provide shelter and food for a wealth of marine life, dissipate wave energy from storms, and even take up CO_2 from the oceans and atmosphere, reducing global warming and countering ocean acidification. Research has indicated that if 9 per cent of the world's oceans were covered in seaweed farms they could take up as much carbon as is emitted each year, globally, while providing protein for the entire world population.

The list of plus points grows when we look at seaweed from a health perspective. Sedentary lifestyles, sugar and wheat addictions, fast foods and the increasing availability of low-price, high-calorie foods result in a plethora of health issues. In times of crisis we should turn to nature, and no other food group contains the range of vitamins, minerals and other beneficial nutrients found in seaweed, some of which are still being discovered and further explored.

For the Japanese, Chinese and Koreans this awareness of seaweed's exceptionally high concentration of vitamins and minerals is nothing new and it has made up a significant part of their diet for generations. These cultures have developed a deep understanding of the health benefits and culinary characteristics of the different seaweed species, something the rest of the world can draw upon. Seaweeds are now accepted in the West as a true superfood.

The way in which we cook now is incredibly diverse, with influences from every corner of the world teasing our palates on a daily basis, and in recent years we have become used to experimenting and more willing to try out new flavours and culinary methods. Cooking with seaweed offers a fabulous opportunity to take this epicurean openness a step futher, bringing new tastes and textures to the table while at the same time nourishing our bodies with a natural product that has been harvested in a sustainable way. Moreover, given the rise in popularity of vegan and vegetarian diets, it is well worth noting how seaweeds can be used as a substitute for more common animal-derived products – from the smoky flavours of dulse, which are not dissimilar to bacon, and the thickening qualities of carrageen, which make it a splendid alternative to gelatine and eggs, to the umami richness of flavour that kelp gives to a stock – with a definite hint of the sea – which makes it the perfect alternative to fish sauce in Thai curries.

Drawing upon all of these attributes, this book contains a collection of recipes that have been adapted to make the very most of these diverse and nutritionally wonderful macro algae, ranging from soups, salads, appetizers and main dishes to sides and salads, dips, desserts, bakes and drinks. Some feature seaweed in the starring role, but many simply show how you can more subtly incorporate it into your diet by using it in familiar, much-loved dishes. From moreish seaweed crisps through to curries and chocolate mousse, there are plenty of exciting and delicious recipes that will leave you eager to get picking, cooking and feasting well into the future! I guess what we are trying to say is that seaweeds are pretty amazing. So pick up your bucket, scissors, pots and pans, and let the seaweed adventure begin...

SAFETY NOTE Seaweed is one of the healthiest ingredients in the world to enjoy, but please refer to the guidelines on safe foraging on page 60, and the important dietary advice on iodine and heavy metals on pages 18 and 288, before you get started.

A HISTORY OF USING SEAWEED

Seaweed has for centuries been used in various ways by many cultures around the world – as tools and ornaments, for rituals, or as a treatment for health problems. However, only a small percentage of the world's civilizations have realised the full potential of seaweed and used it as a food source. Those who have range from the Inuit and Inca to Japanese and Irish, all of whom have relied on seaweeds as an important part of their diets over the years and have paved the way for what we are now experiencing as the seaweed revolution.

Archaeological remains reveal that seaweed was included in the diets of ancient communities who lived near the coast of Chile as far back as 14,000 years ago. This practice wasn't confined to coastal peoples, however, with evidence showing that the indigenous people of the South American Andes, situated far from the ocean, used to buy seaweed from traders and hang it round their necks. This supplied them with a source of beneficial nutrients while they were working in the fields, and demonstrates their awareness of its nutritional value long before scientific research could back it up with proof.

Elsewhere, seaweed was used for similar purposes. The Inuit derived most of their vitamin C from seaweed, while dried dulse was used in Canada and Iceland by the coastal natives as a sniffing tobacco, and historically in the treatment of scurvy. In Ancient Egypt, Cleopatra was said to have bathed in seaweed to promote youthfulness, and in Ancient Greece, Theophrastus mentioned it in his texts.

Asia in particular has harnessed the beneficial properties of seaweed for centuries. Its use in Japan dates back to at least 600BCE, during which time it was classified as a food suitable for a king, and it has also been extensively employed by the Chinese, who have long known that some species, such as *Laminaria* and *Saccharina*, can be used to treat certain diseases. Japan is currently the world's greatest consumer, getting through on average 1.6kg (3½lb) dried seaweed per person per year, with nori being the most-eaten type.

Seaweed use in Europe, particularly in Ireland and Scotland, also stretches back a long way. The Scottish crofters, for instance, used to feed their sheep with sugar kelp, since it made the animals' meat

THE ORIGINS OF UMAMI

The kelp family is probably most renowned for its unique effect on the tastebuds, known as umami. The word umami comes from Japan and is translated as 'pleasant savoury taste'. More than a hundred years ago, a chemist in Tokyo honed in on the taste found in various foods, such as asparagus, cheese, wild mushrooms and meat, but most noticeably dashi – a stock made with kelp that forms the base of miso and a variety of other traditional Japanese dishes – and discovered that it comes from an amino acid known as glutamic acid, which he went on to develop into monosodium glutamate, MSG or E621.

sweeter. Scottish children chewed kelp stipes to clean and strengthen their teeth, while in Ireland dulse was sold as a cure for hangovers. Even earlier in history, it is believed that Greek and Roman soldiers and sailors used seaweed to bandage and treat their wounds and burns, and the Greeks fed seaweed to their livestock as early as 100BCE. All across the Mediterranean since pre-Christian times certain seaweeds were used as a medicine to treat parasitic worms and as a dying agent.

In the past, Ireland, Wales and Scotland have all had much closer relationships with seaweeds than England. This is partly due to the extended periods of hardship and famine in those countries that forced the people to look for alternative food sources, as well as to the legal rights of access to the foreshore that are required in England and made foraging there more tricky. That said, it is the South West of England as well as Wales

Opposite: Dried flaked seaweed is one of the most accessible forms for use in cooking, since it doesn't require any soaking.
Below: Seaweeds are as varied in their tastes, textures and uses as they are in their appearance.

that is famous for laverbread – a seaside delicacy that requires the seaweed to be boiled for hours – which has been enjoyed by the Welsh and Devonians for centuries and remains a favourite today.

Away from the table, washed-up seaweed was traditionally used by farmers in Cornwall as a fertiliser for the land – a horticultural trend that continues nationwide to this day. Having been harvested along the shore, the seaweed was then carted up the steep cliffs by donkeys, a process that is in part responsible for the creation of some coastal paths that still exist.

These days, the immense seaweed resource that thrives in British waters is finally being more fully embraced and understood by cooks. Influenced initially by Asian cuisine, seaweed is now making its mark on the mainstream culinary scene, featuring on the menus at top-end established restaurants and up-and-coming pop-up venues alike, as well as in home kitchens. No longer is seaweed considered an odd choice – it is a sought-after ingredient that bring vibrant colour, unusual tastes and varied flavours to any meal.

SEAWEED CULTIVATION

In countries where seaweed is a diet staple, such as in the Far East, ecologically sound harvesting of wild stock is now not possible because demand far outstrips sustainable supply. Unfortunately, many places have realised this too late and a great number of wild seaweed beds have been depleted, leaving those countries to rely almost solely on seaweed that is cultivated on a large scale. Moreover, as seaweed is gaining in popularity in new territories, so its cultivation and seaweed farming is increasing around the world from Chile and the USA to the UK and Europe.

Seaweed cultivation in the East

Producing by far the most seaweed in Asia, China cultivates about 10–12 million tons wet weight of kelp or kombu annually, as well as smaller quantities of wakame, sargassum, nori and a couple of other species. Of this, about 70 per cent is consumed, with the rest being used as agar, in beauty products, as soil conditioner, as animal feed and to make paper, among other things.

There are two ways in which kelp can be cultivated. One is the hanging kelp-rope cultivation method, often referred to as single-raft cultivation, which is most suited to areas with clearer water. The technique involves suspending vertical ropes from a floating line, weighting them down with a small stone, and allowing the seaweed to develop around the tensioned lines – resulting in something similar to natural kelp forests. This enables greater free-flow of water around the algae, but often the growth is uneven and can be difficult to predict. The other method is the horizontal kelp rope, which is also called double-raft cultivation. The floating line is about 60m (197ft) long and is anchored at one end to the sea bed, with the rest floating on the water's surface, aided by buoys. This method gives more even growth of kelp but is resistant to water motion and may impede the free movement of marine life in the area.

Below: Seaweed farms are common in China and other Far Eastern countries; laminaria, a kelp, is the most-cultivated variety.

In Japan, nori is a staple food and as such has been cultivated for centuries. However, with the recent rise in popularity of sushi and interest in health foods in general across the world, nori cultivation has become an ever-more lucrative business for seaweed farmers, with the government sponsoring the maintenance of prefectorial seedling centres. These are places where the seaweed is grown indoors in tanks, on ropes of shells that are suspended from bamboo sticks placed lengthways just above the water level. Once established, these curtains of seaweed are then placed in the sea. It's all a serious business, involving purpose-built rooms to control the light intensity and produce the highest-quality seaweed.

Despite the established nature and efficiency of these Eastern seaweed farms, however, concerns about the Fukushima disaster and water quality, coupled with rising export fees and a growing commitment to localism, are causing people outside Asia to look to new methods for cultivating seaweed closer to home.

Seaweed farming in the West

Currently, the seaweed we harvest from the shores of Cornwall is hand cut, using scissors, from its natural environment. We do this to ensure that the seaweed has the opportunity to regenerate, thus supporting its sustainability and avoiding harming the marine environment – something we will always prioritise. We also have the correct licence.

This tradition of harvesting naturally occurring seaweed is nothing new, but then neither is its cultivation; in the past, stones were planted within ocean beds to encourage the growth of seaweed in coastal areas of Ireland, and this method is now seeing a resurgence.

On a more commercial scale, seaweed 'farming' is an ever-growing trend – something that is not perhaps surprising, given that a Dutch scientist has calculated that a network of seaweed farms covering a mere 180,000 square kilometres (69,500 square miles) would produce sufficient protein to feed the entire global population. Moreover, since these 'sea farms' require no deforestation, no fresh water and no fertilisers – unlike land-based farms – they are a much more sustainable option, and must be considered in the future.

To this end, a number of EU countries has joined forces to develop a textile that can be suspended from a platform in the open sea, upon which seaweed can be cultivated in a more intensive way. This same progress in seaweed cultivation can be seen in the USA, too, where dedicated seaweed farms are starting to appear in

Above: Nori is a common ingredient in Japan, where it is sold in vast quantities in both its dry and fresh forms.

places such as Maine, and seaweed is now being cultivated alongside shellfish, for instance in some oyster farms in Long Island Sound.

This rise in seaweed farming has manifold benefits, since in addition to providing food, more widespread seaweed cultivation could also benefit the ocean and the planet at large, since seaweed can help absorb waste nutrients from fish farms and excess CO_2 from both the air and water, as well as creating a habitat for fish and shellfish.

Given the benefits of seaweed as a source of food and energy, and as a carbon sink that could help soak up excess emissions, it is probable that it will, and should, become a much more common foodstuff – which is why we want to share these recipes and provide an accessible guide to how to use it.

THE ECOLOGY OF SEAWEED

Seaweeds are more remarkable than you might at first think. They have been around for a very, very long time, with the earliest fossil records stemming from over 1 billion years ago, well before the more familiar daffodil or marigold evolved. Growing in some of the most challenging environments on earth, seaweeds have to cope on a daily basis with surging tides, battering storms and grazing. On top of that, they need to withstand rapid desiccation, extreme temperature fluctuations, intense UV exposure, considerable changes in salinity, and powerful waves that try to rip them to pieces.

It should come as no surprise, therefore, that over time they have evolved and developed some remarkable strategies to face these challenges – from rubbery stipes (the equivalent of the stem) and gel-coated fronds and blades (the equivalent of leaves) that dissipate wave energy, to water-retaining hydrocolloids that prevent desiccation. These remarkable algae also contain high levels of of vitamins and iodine that help fight viral and bacterial infections, and some types even secrete a natural sunscreen that protects them from damaging UV radiation. It is no wonder that seaweeds are a useful addition to our diet!

'Seaweed' is the collective term for marine macro-algae, or large algae that live in the ocean. There are about 10,000 seaweed species in the world, which can be separated in three different groups: red (7,000 worldwide, around 340 in Britain), green (1,500 worldwide, around 100 in Britain) and brown seaweeds (2,000 worldwide, around 185 in Britain). The term seaweed is really all they have in common, however: brown and green/red seaweeds differ from each other as much as animals do from plants.

The red and green seaweeds are distant cousins and form part of the plant kingdom, while the brown seaweeds are a different kettle of fish altogether, because they split from a common ancestor earlier in their evolutionary history. Moreover, while the green and red seaweeds are rather small, the brown seaweeds tend to be much larger, with the brown giant kelp reaching a staggering 70m (230ft) in length.

The colour variations of the three groups arises from the different pigments that fulfil the same role as chlorophyll, the pigment that gives plants their green colour – namely absorbing energy from (sun)light. All three types of seaweed contain some green chlorophyll, but the red and brown seaweeds also contain other pigments that mask the green colour.

The large brown seaweeds are probably the most important from an ecological perspective. They are certainly the most abundant and some species, such as kelp, can form large forests that absorb large quantities of CO_2 as well as providing a unique habitat and food source for a wide range of marine organisms including fish, sea urchins, lobsters, sea otters and myriad crustaceans and other small creatures.

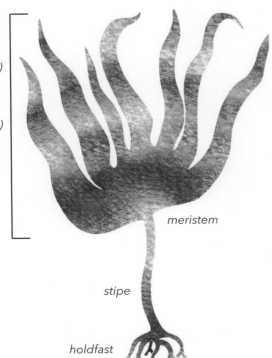

blade
(brown
seaweeds)

frond
(green
and red
seaweeds)

meristem

stipe

holdfast

COLOUR-SHIFTING SEAWEED

When you put any brown seaweed in hot, almost boiling water it changes colour and turns ... green! Put red dulse in hot water and it turns ... brown! Put green seaweed in hot water and ... nothing happens (well, it does become hot). The reason for the colour change is that the pigments masking the green pigment present in all three types is broken down, making the other pigments visible.

Zonation

The keen observer quickly notices that different species of seaweed are distributed at different heights above the shore. This zonation happens because the species located in each are best adapted to the microclimate in that zone and have a more optimal growth there than do other species. This does not mean that the faster a seaweed species can grow the more successful it is. More important is how well it is adapted to the conditions in which it grows. Seaweed that grows deep in the ocean, below the intertidal, has to be very good at converting the reduced intensity and frequency of sunlight into energy. Having the ability to withstand desiccation due to dropping tides is not so important.

The zonation that occurs in the intertidal reflects the degree of desiccation (time out of the water) a seaweed can withstand, with species that can cope with longer periods out of the water growing higher up the shore. Other environmental variables that

Below: This chart shows how different seaweeds may be distributed according to tidal range along a particular shoreline.

Above: Hardy seaweeds, such as gutweed, are among the few that can survive in the splash zone.
Right: Knowing which seaweeds grow in which zones will allow you to forage more effectively for the type you are after.

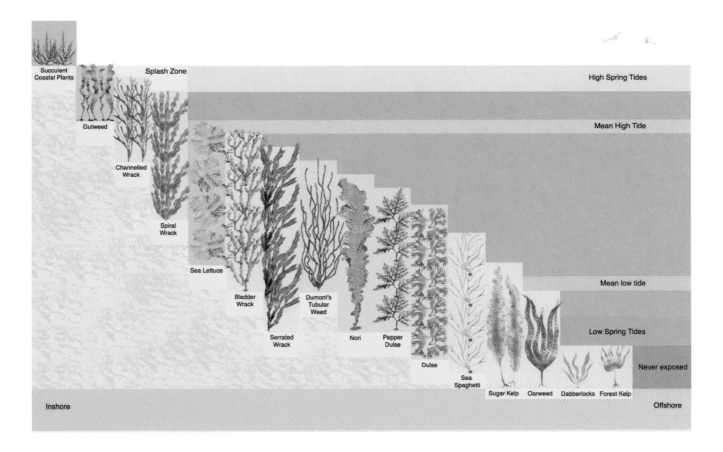

impact where different seaweeds grow include exposure to waves, nutrient content, turbidity, water flow, oxygen levels and salinity. However, all species require the same basic ingredients to grow: light, nutrients and sea water. It is for these reasons that you find seaweeds only in the shallower parts of the ocean, where enough light penetrates the water to the seabed to allow them to convert solar energy into energy to grow and reproduce.

The different places in which seaweeds grow need some explanation, since this will enable you to predict where to find them. These places can be divided in two main zones, the intertidal and the subtidal, but there is also a splash zone.

Intertidal zone

The intertidal is the area of the shore that is under water at the highest tide and out of the water at the lowest tide. The intertidal zone is also known as the foreshore, seashore or littoral zone and can be further broken down into the upper shore, the middle shore and the lower shore.

Seaweeds' adaptation to different climatic conditions is best shown in the intertidal zone, which is characterised by different levels of tidal inundation. The upper shore has a finer selection of seaweeds which are shorter and lighter. As you move down towards the

lower shore the seaweeds become hardier, thicker and heavier until you reach the dense kelps forests of the lower shore and beyond. These characteristics enable them to thrive in their given zones.

The upper shore is the zone at the upper limit of the high tide. It is only submerged for a few hours a day and is dominated by periwinkles, barnacles, limpets and encrusting lichens. Only the few types of seaweed that can withstand prolonged periods of desiccation, such as channelled wrack and egg wrack, grow here.

The middle shore is the main strip in the intertidal that is uncovered and covered by water at every tide. This is the largest stretch of the intertidal and is characterised by different types of wrack, dulse, sea lettuce, gutweed and pepper dulse. Other marine organisms include barnacles, limpets, mussels, crabs and anemones.

The lower shore is the zone that is exposed during and around the extreme low spring tides that occur a few days each month. It is characterised by kelps (kombu or oarweed), Irish moss and common coralweed. As you look at the sea shore on a very low spring tide you can clearly make out the different types of seaweeds growing in the different zones.

Subtidal

The area below the intertidal is called the subtidal, or sublittoral, zone. This is the region that is always submerged and where sunlight can still reach the ocean floor. This is dominated by kelp forests in the shallower parts. Where not enough light penetrates the seabed for kelps to grow, small red seaweeds dominate.

Splash zone

This zone is located just above the upper shore. Although seaweeds cannot grow here and it is only immersed every now and again at spring tides during storms, it regularly receives salt-water spray. It is characterised by lichens, such as the black tar lichen, since these are among the few organisms that can survive the harsh conditions.

Seaweed grazers

In the same way that land vegetables and other plants are consumed by a variety of insects and invertebrates, so are seaweeds by their marine equivalents. We can distinguish five different types of grazers:

Molluscs such as topshell snails, periwinkles and limpets are abundant grazers of seaweed and are omnipresent in gutweed, sea lettuce, dulse, the various different wracks, Irish moss and nori, where they hide from predators. They mostly feed on microscopically small young seaweeds and microalgae by scraping the rock surface.

The large kelps and sea spaghetti are not affected by molluscs. Instead, they are eaten by blue-rayed limpets. Not a true limpet, these small creatures, about 5mm (⅕in) in length, are more abundant in autumn and are mostly present on the divide between the stipe and blade of kelp and also the lower parts of sea-spaghetti fronds. They slowly eat a hole in the stipes and fronds of the seaweeds, which can potentially weaken them so much that they break off in heavy waves. Blue-rayed limpets are difficult to remove, so harvesting of the species they favour is generally best done early in the season before they have a chance to take hold.

Isopods are marine crustaceans that, like snails, feed on seaweeds and are also common in gutweed, sea lettuce, dulse, the different wracks, Irish moss and nori. They are small invertebrates that resemble woodlice (and indeed are related to them) and the species you will find on seaweed are generally not bigger than 2cm (⅘in). They are well camouflaged and only when dried or cooked will they become more visible, when they turn orange,

like cooked shrimp. You could pick off and discard these critters, but why go through the hassle? Like prawns or shrimp, they are very tasty. In fact, we eat them sun-dried as a mini-snack!

Sea urchins feed mainly on brown kelps. They can be a problem because when their natural predators are absent they can cause entire kelp forests to disappear.

Some manatees, especially the ones in Florida, are known to eat seaweeds, even though their diet normally mostly consists of sea grasses (which are not closely related to seaweeds).

And then there is a sixth type of grazer: us humans. That is, those of us who eat seaweed…

Above: Molluscs such as snails are voracious grazers of seaweed, and also use the underwater foliage as cover to hide them from predators.
Opposite: The middle shore is the region of the shoreline where the greatest number of seaweed species grow.

HEALTH AND NUTRITION

The fact that seaweeds are good for health is not news: the Japanese have long attributed healing properties to them and have used seaweed (mainly kelp) extracts to treat a variety of ailments including goitre, tumours and worms. The Romans are thought to have used seaweed to treat wounds, burns and rashes and the Irish have for centuries been making a seaweed tea from Irish moss as a remedy against the common cold and hangovers. The Inuit get an important portion of their vitamin C from brown seaweeds.

It is only recently, though, that the mechanisms behind these properties have been researched, backing up traditional knowledge with scientific reasoning and explaining how exactly seaweed benefits us. For instance, it has been proven that dulse, the seaweed traditionally used as a cure for worms, contains kainic acid, which does indeed kill intestinal parasites. Moreover, recent UK research indicates that compounds in seaweed inhibit the absorption of fat and carbohydrates in our bodies, meaning it can thus start to play an important role in combating obesity and aiding weight loss, of course as part of a healthy diet. That said, studies into the effect of seaweeds on human health are still scarce and need to be further substantiated.

Minerals

Minerals play an important role in the functioning and building of our bodies, each one fulfilling one or more key roles, so it is essential we include an adequate amount and range in our diets.

Seaweeds are rich in many different minerals and often contain them in quantities greatly exceeding those of land plants. For example, dulse, sea lettuce and gutweed contain over 25 per cent more iron than meat; arame and wakame contain 10 times more calcium than milk; and dulse contains more vitamin C than oranges. However we generally consume smaller quantities of seaweed in the context of a recipe.

Seaweeds absorb these and other minerals directly from the ocean, and then concentrate them according to the plant's specific needs. The minerals found in seaweed in the largest quantities are calcium, phosphorus, iodine, magnesium, iron, potassium and sodium, but there are many more present in smaller quantities.

Calcium

Calcium is important in the formation and growth of strong teeth and bones. It helps prevent osteoporosis and arthritis and plays a key role in muscle growth and contraction, blood clotting and regulation of the heart. Most seaweeds are high in calcium.

Iodine

Of all the seaweeds, the brown ones are richest in iodine. This is present in all our cells and, although we only need it in small quantities, it plays an important role in maintaining a healthy thyroid. Too much can result in a hyperactive thyroid, which could accelerate the metabolism, causing (unhealthy) weight loss, a rapid or irregular heartbeat, sweating, nervousness or irritability. On the other hand, iodine deficiency can result in underactive thyroid function, potentially causing weight gain, depression, constipation, poor ability to tolerate cold, and tiredness.

In some countries, there is a high level of iodine deficiency, mostly due to the reduction of dairy and seafood consumption. Vegetarians and vegans are especially at risk, since, apart from seaweed, animal sources are the major way in which we obtain it, so eating some seaweed can certainly be of benefit. That said, if you suffer from a thyroid disorder – hyper- or hypothyroidism for instance – it is best to consult your doctor before including seaweed in your diet.

Even if you don't have a problem with your thyroid, you need to be aware that some seaweeds contain exceptionally high levels of iodine, and care needs to be taken not to consume too much of these. Kelp in particular should be eaten in moderation, since this contains the highest levels of iodine found in any food.

The content of iodine in seaweeds can, however, be lowered. Boiling, steaming or toasting all reduce the iodine content by 20–99 per cent and some of it evaporates during the drying process. Alternatively, you prefer to eat seaweed raw, simply soak it in cold water for about 30 minutes to reduce its iodine content.

Copper

Copper is necessary to regulate enzymatic processes that help protect against infections, including rheumatism, arthritis and skin diseases. Green and red seaweeds tend to be higher in copper than brown ones.

DID YOU KNOW?

One of the reasons sea air has such a beneficial influence on us is the fact that it contains iodine. By breathing in the sea air we also absorb iodine!

Opposite: Mighty seaweed packs an impressive nutritional punch.

Iron

Iron is needed to create red blood cells. It helps to transport oxygen through our body, improves circulation, prevents headaches, improves concentration and increases sex drive. Green seaweeds are generally higher in iron than red ones, which are in turn higher in iron than brown ones.

Magnesium

Magnesium is needed for making strong teeth and bones. Moreover, it helps avoid muscle spasms and cramp and can improve sleep, and can also help asthma and diabetes. Green seaweeds tend to be highest in magnesium.

Potassium

Potassium plays a vital role in cell communication and the correct functioning of the nervous system, and it also helps clean the kidneys and reduces psychological tension. Red and brown seaweeds are highest in potassium.

Zinc

Zinc prevents and heals infections and skin diseases and supports the metabolism, and is also vital for the formation of healthy reproductive organs. Nori is an especially good source, although most seaweeds contain some zinc.

Above: Seaweeds can be used fresh or dried, as the main ingredient or a subtle seasoning, in a variety of different recipes from soups to desserts.

Vitamins

Seaweeds also contain a large number of vitamins but it is the red and green types that have the widest range. There is quite a lot of discrepancy in the vitamin content between different seaweeds, and within species this also varies per season. Any nutritional values you see on packets are therefore averages or typical values.

One vitamin that is of particular interest is vitamin B12, or cobalamin, which is mostly found in its naturally occuring state in meat. Natural vegetarian options that contain it include milk, yogurt, cheese and eggs, but for vegans seaweed is pretty much the only source (specifically dulse, nori, gutweed and sea lettuce). You can also find vitamin B12 in some processed foods such as breakfast cereals, soy milk and yeast extract, but these are fortified with the vitamin, rather than it being naturally occurring.

Other beneficial properties

Seaweed is not only rich in vitamins and minerals, but it also – perhaps more importantly – contains many other compounds that have anti-oxidative properties and can play an important role in the prevention of diseases and keeping the body healthy.

While the red and green seaweeds may pack a punch when it comes to vitamins and minerals, it is the brown seaweeds that are alginate champions. Some of these, such as fucoidan, have also been shown to have anti-tumour properties. This has been tested through epidemiological studies in the Japanese, who eat on average 14g (½oz) of seaweed per day. Their rates of certain types of cancer, such as breast cancer, are dramatically lower than those in nations that don't eat seaweed.

Many of these compounds fall under the name of complex sulphated polysaccharides, of which there are many types in seaweed, all with different properties. These include prebiotic advantages, which means they promote the growth of beneficial microorganisms in the gut. Some names that these polysaccharides go by are alginate, ulvan, carrageenan and laminaran. They are found in the different seaweeds as follows:

- **In brown seaweeds** Alginates, laminarins, fucans, cellulose, fucoidan
- **In green seaweeds** Ulvan
- **In red seaweeds** Agar, carrageenan

Alginates are responsible for making seaweeds slimy. They dissolve in water and form a gel that keeps the seaweed moist – a useful survival mechanism that is helpful when the tide goes out. Because of these hydrocolloid (literally 'water-gluing') properties of alginates they are widely used in the pharmaceutical, food and medical industries.

Agar is a gelatinous substance with a wide range of industrial applications, including as a thickener for soups, fruit preserves and ice cream; as a clarifying agent in brewing; and for sizing paper and fabrics. In the food industry it is classified as food additive (E406). As a solid substrate it also used as a culture medium in microbiological work.

Fibre

Fibre forms an important part of our diets, even though we do not actually digest it. It comes in two forms: soluble and insoluble. Soluble fibre slows digestion, thereby lowering cholesterol and blood-sugar levels, and keeps us feeing fuller for longer. Insoluble fibre makes food heavier and enables it to move through the intestines more easily, which helps with digestion.

Seaweed is full of fibre, and it is an equal or better source of it than food grown on land. For instance, kelp contains about 2.5g per 40g wet weight in total fibre, whereas brown rice contains just 1.8g and peas 1.5g.

Protein

Protein is essential for the healthy functioning of the body, yet all too often in the West it is eaten in meat form. Although meat, eaten in moderation, provides a range of beneficial nutrients, the over-consumption of red meat in particular is linked to a number of health problems, such as heart disease and cancer, as well as complex and numerous environmental issues. It is important, then, that we utilise vegetable sources and reduce our reliance on animal protein, and seaweed is one way of doing this.

Red seaweeds, and especially dulse and laver, are rich sources of protein. Dulse contains between 9 and 25 per cent protein, depending upon the season, with seaweed picked in the winter generally containing the highest levels. Laver has an amino-acid profile that is similar to that of soya beans and other leguminous sources of protein, yet with none of the environmental drawbacks.

It is thought that alongside the protein, seaweeds contain beneficial bioactive peptides that may help to reduce high blood pressure and prevent cardiovascular disease.

SEAWEEDS AND HEAVY METALS

The reason why seaweeds are such a good source of minerals is that they are very effectively able to 'absorb' them from seawater and concentrate them. The downside is that, along with the beneficial minerals, they also act like a sponge and take in a number of heavy metals that pollute waterways – indeed, some marine ecologists use seaweeds as a way to monitor levels of pollutants in the water. Of these heavy metals, arsenic is the most problematic and poses the greatest toxicity risk. It has been found in most seaweed species, but of particular concern is hijiki, and many countries, including England, Canada and New Zealand, now recommend that you do not eat it, unless is comes from a verifiable certified organic source.

OTHER USES FOR SEAWEED

We mainly harvest food-grade seaweed that we sell to surfside cafes, restaurants and food shacks, as well as to home cooks who are keen to get their daily dose of Vitamin Sea! However, as we have already seen, it also has many uses in the food industry, particularly as a gelling agent in foods such as ice cream. Outside the home and industrial kitchen, its soothing and nourishing properties make it popular in the cosmetic industry, too, and due to its high nutrient content it can also be used as animal food and fertiliser. Seaweed is versatile stuff.

Beauty and bath

As surfers, we know that getting out of the sea always leaves our bodies feeling refreshed and invigorated. This is in part due to the way in which we reconnect with the elements that created us. Given that life evolved from water and we all originated in the sea it makes sense to us to bathe in the very elements that made us by adding seaweed or sea salts to our bath water.

Our predilection for bringing the sea into our bathrooms is nothing new. Seaweeds such as kelp and bladderwrack have been popular ingredients for beauty treatments since Babylonian times, and Japanese onsen (hot springs) were often laden with seaweed, which releases its restorative gels into the water, toning skin while nourishing and moisturising it. It also stimulates the glandular system.

When you consider that ageing is caused by poor oxygenation, it's no surprise that those of us who get in the sea may appear younger and have brighter skin. We are reversing the ageing process by regulating skin cells' oxygen intake when we expose it to seaweed. Fortunately, even if you live inland, you can get the stimulating effects of the sea by snipping some seaweed into your bath.

In beauty salons, or even at home, seaweed is the key ingredient of treatments such as thalassotherapy or seaweed wraps. This involves placing seaweed on the skin, whereupon the natural gel it exudes tightens and moisturises the skin while at the same time releasing nourishing minerals such as magnesium, potassium and iodide.

Seaweed's coagulant properties make it an important ingredient in other cosmetic items, too, such as toothpaste, shampoos and creams, wherein it acts as a stabiliser, in much the same way as it does for some foods.

You can make your own treatments if you have access to a beach. Anything within reach will be safe to use, although you may want to rinse off the crustaceans that have hopped along for the ride!

Below: Seaweed has long been harnessed as a beauty aid, and it is very easy to use: simply pop some in your bath, lie back and soak it up!

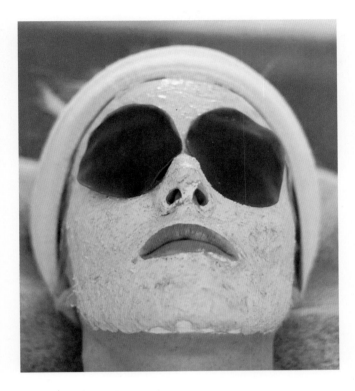

Sea lettuce face mask

Sea lettuce is a seaweed that is easy to obtain because it is often found floating around in rock pools. Unlike kelp, it is a thin seaweed that also grows in very large sheets. This means it can easily be manipulated to fit the shape of the face, where it will impart its minerals on to the skin's surface.

1   Take one sheet of sea lettuce and wash it in clean water to remove any sand and livestock. If you dry it out, fold it to help retain its shape.
2   When you rehydrate the sea lettuce, do so in cold water.
3   As it becomes pliable, cover the entire face with the green sheet and relax for 10–15 minutes, while the seaweed releases its minerals.
4   Rinse and then implement your daily skincare routine.

Seaweed body scrub

Seaweed is widely available in powder form and makes an excellent addition to this scrub, which freshens and moisturises the skin. Meanwhile, adzuki beans – which have long been used in Japanese cosmetics for their saponin content – removes excess oils, while oats are soothing for the skin and the almond acts as an exfoliant and moisturiser. Use this as a scrub two or three times a week to give your skin a deep cleanse and leave it feeling refreshed and revitalised.

30ml/2 tbsp dried adzuki beans
  (available from health-food stores)
30ml/2 tbsp ground almonds
30ml/2 tbsp ground oats
30ml/2 tbsp ground seaweed (we recommend kelp)
15ml/1 tbsp honey
a few drops of your favourite essential oils (see Tip overleaf)

1   Grind the adzuki beans using a coffee grinder or blender. You can sift the powder to remove the larger grains. Transfer the powder to a bowl.
2   Blend the ground almonds and oats in the blender or coffee grinder. If they are still a little coarse, this won't a problem as they will have gentle exfoliating properties. Add to the ground adzuki beans along with the ground seaweed.
3   Mix all ingredients together in a bowl and store the mixture in a small glass mason or Kilner jar.
4   When you are ready to use the scrub, mix a small bean-sized amount in your hand with the honey and enough water to form a paste. Spread this over your face using small circular movements, leave for a few minutes, then rinse with water.

Above: To really maximise the beauty benefits of seaweed, slap on some seaweed scrub or face pack, apply some kelp eye patches, and relax.

Alternatively, if you don't live near the sea, keep your eyes peeled for fresh seaweed in supermarkets or have a go at rehydrating kelp. Here are some home DIY projects that you can do to feel the many benefits of bathing with seaweed.

Fucus bath

Take two handfuls of bladderwrack from the shore and rinse to remove sand and debris. Throw it into a warm bath and feel the fronds unfurl and enrich the water. Alternatively, you can purchase reusable Fucus bath bags, which add their nourishing gel to the bath water, and can be rubbed on to the skin as a soothing exfoliator.

Kelp eye patches

Whether caused by burning the candle at both ends or suffering from hay fever, these little patches will help soothe irritated or tired eyes as well as tightening skin and reducing inflammation or puffiness.

1   Take a strip of dried kelp and at its widest point cut a length measuring about 10cm (4in). Fold it in half.
2   Cut a rough circle from the kelp. Voilà! You have two little soothing patches to place over your eyes.

Tip: The seaweed can be quite pungent, so to make it smell nicer you can add essential oils. These bring additional benefits, as outlined below:

Lavender – Tones and revitalises problem skin
Rose geranium – Balances oil production and helps remove oil from clogged pores
Sweet orange – Soothing for acne-prone skin and a tonic for mature skin
Tea tree – Balances oil production and helps clear or prevent breakouts, as well as being antibacterial

Healthcare

Seaweed species have been employed in Eastern medicine for thousands of years. Used to treat tuberculosis, parasites, colds and flu, as well as rheumatism, wounds and even cancer, seaweed is revered as a health food. When we consider that the ocean is where life began, it is perhaps not surprising that taking minerals from that very source may help to restore health.

In order to better understand the science behind these centuries-old observations, laboratories worldwide are conducting studies into the various benefits of seaweed and extracting the key health-supporting components. One such constituent is the mineral iodine, which as already discussed is commonly considered essential for the healthy functioning of the thyroid. Research is also underway to identify the antiseptic and antimicrobial properties of seaweed.

Moreover, the emulsifying properties of seaweed are just as useful in modern medicine as they are in the food and cosmetics industries. From dental moulds to medical creams and pastes, and from the soluble outer shell of capsules to wound dressings, the alginates in seaweed have a range of uses in healthcare.

Gelling agents

Similar in structure to gelatine, the hydrogels present within different varieties of seaweed make them useful vegetarian alternatives to gelatine. Carageenan and agar, for example, are used as gelling agents in many vegetarian sweet products, and alginate is also popular as a thickener or stabiliser, as discussed on page 21. Sodium alginate has recently become popular within the molecular gastronomy food sector for its part in the process of spherification. Chefs such as Heston Blumenthal and those who follow in his footsteps have employed this food-preparation technique to create tiny balls of flavour, akin to bath pearls. Its properties are useful for ensuring that food retains its shape, and as such it can be used as an additive in foods such as pasta.

Not limited to the food industry, sodium alginate is also used in textiles, as well as in coatings for paper and in adhesives. You can even get seaweed furniture created from Fucus harvested from the Danish coast. This common brown algae, often referred to as bladderwrack, can be found on many coasts and is rich in alginate,

Below: You can add different types of essential oil to your seaweed scrub according to your skin type or just your preference for scent.

which, once dried, ground up and cooked, forms a gluey substance that dries to resemble cork. The abundance of salt in the seaweed then helps to preserve the moulded, fire-resistant furniture, which will eventually biodegrade and can go on to be used as fertiliser on the land. In homage to the coastline that seaweed symbolises, many designers use the sea and the natural world as their inspiration when using this material.

All in all, it's pretty marvellous stuff, when you consider you can eat it, sit on it and heal cuts with it too!

Fertiliser and animal food

Fittingly for a region that is as famous for its fecund fields and farming as its fish, Cornwall is one of many coastal areas worldwide that utilises seaweed as a fertiliser. Elsewhere, the practice can be traced back to the 14th century in France and Iceland, where seaweeds were and are collected from the beach and spread directly on the fields so that the nutrients can filter down into the soil, but it occurs in other places too.

These days, granulated powders and liquids made from extracts of brown algae are readily available in garden centres and online, providing a nutrient boost to the soil that means plants grow bigger and healthier. Moreover, some reports suggest that applying seaweed also protects plants from frost and decreases their chance of infestation. Those following an organic growing regime may choose to spread unprocessed seaweed on beds when growing vegetables such as asparagus and cabbage, though it is advisable in these instances to reduce the salinity of the seaweed first by washing it in rain water.

Above: The rugged coastlines of Scotland are rich habitats for seaweed, which is harvested and used to feed man, beast and land.

At The Cornish Seaweed Company, we make our own plant feed by saving the water that is the by-product of rehydrating our sea spaghetti and dulse, and using it on domestic plants and vegetable beds, and you can do this too – nothing need go to waste.

Seaweed can also be fed to domestic animals, something that is reflected in the colloquial names for some species: for instance, dulse is named 'cow weed' in England, and 'seaderlil' or 'horse seaweed' in Lapland and Norway. Animals naturally eat the green stuff, so it makes sense that farmers have long been using it; texts dating back to the 1st century CE cite seaweed as animal food in the Mediterranean. Abundant and full of nutrients, it is especially beneficial in regions with depleted grasslands, which is likely to be why Scandinavian countries such as Norway and Iceland fed their cattle on it during the Middle Ages. Today, the practice still continues in places such as along the shoreline of western Scotland, where sheep graze on Fucus – which is reported to lend the meat an umami quality and make it sweeter.

Back in the water, seaweed provides both food and shelter for fish, who in turn play a part in the macro algaes' propagation. And these aren't the only benefits – fish, especially farmed ones, that eat a diet high in seaweeds have lower mortality rates, fewer infections and are richer in omega oils, as well as being bigger and reportedly having a better flavour. This makes seaweed a good choice for fish farms, and companies now make complex, nutritious farmed-fish food using seaweed from around the world.

THE SEAWEEDS

There are thousands of seaweeds in the world, of which only a few hundred can be found in Britain. Many of these seaweeds are either very small, are so rare that they are hardly encountered, or look so similar to each other that they can only be distinguished with the help of a microscope. Below, you can find a description of the seaweeds that are most easily encountered. Most of these are edible and many are not confined to the UK. In fact, some can be found in large parts of the Atlantic, such as the kelps (many *Laminaria* species) and dulse, and others such as sea lettuce have an almost global distribution.

Sea lettuce

Sea lettuce is probably the best-known green seaweed and is often known as sea greens. It grows explosively in the warm summer months then, in autumn, the fronds die off. In some sheltered bays with nutrient-rich waters it can form dense floating communities that, combined with warmer seawater, create 'green tides'. These can cover entire beaches and shores, forming a thick, smelly, decaying layer that is most definitely not edible!

Also known as: Sea greens, sea salad, glasán, green laver

Botanical name: *Ulva lactuca*. (There are at least four species of sea lettuce identified so far in the UK and Ireland, however they are very hard to tell apart, and in practical terms *Ulva* can refer to any species.)

Colour: Light to dark green

Description: As the name might suggest, sea lettuce looks like salad. It has large, thin but tough green fronds that can reach up to 70cm (27½in) long and 30cm (12in) wide. It is quite unmistakable and can sometimes be confused with gutweed, which is thinner and more grass-like (see page 28).

Habitat and distribution: Sea lettuce is very common. It can be found throughout the UK and almost worldwide – in Europe (especially France, the Low Countries and up to Denmark); North America (along the east and west coasts); Central America; the Caribbean Islands; South America; Africa; Indian Ocean Islands; Pacific Islands; China; South-west Asia; Australia and New Zealand. It grows mainly in rock pools and on all levels of the shore, and is prolific in waters that are nutrient-rich, for instance those off the coast of Brittany in France, where there is a high level of nitrates in the water as a result of run-off from intensive farming. It becomes less abundant towards the north.

Harvesting: Cut the frond halfway from late spring to mid-summer, leaving behind the holdfast and some of the frond.

Taste: It has a distinctive salty flavour, with a slightly bitter aftertaste, both of which can be reduced by soaking it in fresh water. Commonly used in soups and salads, or dried and flaked to be used as a seasoning.

Nutritional highlights: High in calcium, copper, iodine, iron, magnesium, manganese, potassium and zinc, and vitamins A, C, E, B2, B9 and B12.

Gutweed

Gutweed is closely related to sea lettuce but is thinner and rather grass-like, with tubular branching fronds. It is treated in much the same way as sea lettuce, and together they are often referred to as sea greens or salad.

Also known as: Sea greens, sea salad, grass kelp, mermaid's hair

Botanical name: *Ulva intestinalis*

Colour: Light to dark green

Description: The blades can grow to over 30cm (12in) long although they are often shorter and hollow and sometimes filled with gas, which makes the seaweed stand upright under water, and resemble the large intestines of mammals, hence the name.

Habitat and distribution: Very similar to sea lettuce, gutweed is found in most places worldwide, but especially in the Baltic and Mediterranean Seas and the Pacific Ocean, and waters around the Azores; Belgium; Denmark; Ireland; Norway; Poland; Russia; Alaska; the Aleutian Islands; Puget Sound; Japan; Korea; Mexico; the Philippines and Israel. It enjoys brackish waters, for instance in areas where there is freshwater run-off from streams or sewage drainage. So, when picking, make sure to get it from unpolluted waters!

Harvesting: Cut the frond halfway, leaving behind the holdfast and some of the frond. It is available year round, but is at its best in late spring and summer.

Taste: Similar to sea lettuce, gutweed has a slightly salty flavour that can be used as a seasoning in breads, omelettes, stir-fries and many other dishes.

Nutritional highlights: High in calcium, copper, iodine, iron, magnesium, manganese, potassium and zinc, and vitamins A, C, E, B2, B9 and B12.

Dulse

Dulse is among the tastiest and best-known edible seaweeds and is going through a real foodie revival, for good reason. Its earliest recorded use was by the monks of St Columba, who harvested it some 1,400 years ago in Scotland, but it was also historically eaten in Iceland, Norway and France. Dulse is probably the most-eaten seaweed in Ireland, where it is sold dried as a snack. The young leaves are also very tasty when eaten raw.

Also known as: Atlantic dulse, water leaf, sheep dulse, shelldulse, duileasc, dillisk, crannogh, creathnach

Botanical name: *Palmaria palmata*

Colour: Dark purple to brown-red. Can turn a lovely shade of pink when dried.

Description: Up to 50cm (20in) in length and only a few millimetres thick. The texture ranges from membrane-thin in the young leaves to leathery in the older leaves, which consist of flattened fronds emanating from a discoid holdfast, often with a small stipe that expands to form simple or palmately divided fronds with distinctive marginal leaflets appearing on older specimens, especially those that have been damaged.

Habitat and distribution: Dulse is a common cold-water species that occurs throughout the UK. It is available from Arctic Russia to Portugal; the Baltic; Arctic Canada to New Jersey (USA); and in Japan and Korea (though this hasn't been officially verified as being the same species). Dulse grows in the intertidal as well as the subtidal zone, where it is often found on the stipes of forest kelp. In the intertidal it prefers more shady areas, where better-quality plants can be located. It grows best on a boulder beach where the boulders provide enough shade. In more exposed shores, undivided or sparsely divided forms grow on mussels. These are considered more tender and palatable in their raw form than those found in more sheltered areas, which tend to be dried and ground.

Harvesting: Dulse is available year round but is best harvested during spring. Cut up to half of the plant, leaving behind enough to grow back. Make sure to remove any snails from in between the fronds since they have a tendency to hold on tightly.

Taste: Rich, salty, umami with a sweet aftertaste, it has been likened to bacon and is traditionally especially appreciated in Ireland, Iceland, Atlantic Canada and north-east USA. Tender young specimens can be eaten raw, but it is generally sold dried.

Nutritional highlights: High in calcium, iron, iodine, copper, manganese, magnesium, potassium and zinc and in vitamins A, B1, B2, B9, B12 and C.

Pepper dulse

Pepper dulse is one of the most wonderful seaweeds to eat. Even though it is quite small – only a few centimetres long – it is probably the most intensely flavoured type around. Dried and powdered, it makes for a fantastic spice. It is easily distinguished from other species, especially by its taste, which cannot be mistaken.

Also known as: Truffle of the sea

Botanical name: *Osmundea pinnatifida*

Colour: Brown/blackish, purple to brownish-red, bleaching to pale yellow fronds, sometimes yellowish-green when found higher up the shore.

Description: A small species, up to 8cm (3⅛in) in length, but generally shorter and broadly rounded in shape, pepper dulse is cartilaginous. The fronds grow very close together and are densely interwoven.

Habitat and distribution: Pepper dulse grows abundantly on open rock surfaces, often in flattened rosettes, in the middle and lower intertidal, as well as in the subtidal. It occurs throughout the UK apart from in the south-east, as well as in parts of Ireland and the Channel Islands. Elsewhere, this and similar species grow in many places around the world, including non-Mediterranean areas of Europe; several Atlantic Islands; tropical and subtropical western Atlantic; the USA (Florida and North Carolina); temperate South America; a few parts of Africa; Cyprus; Turkey; Yemen; Pakistan; India; Korea; Taiwan; Indonesia and the Philippines, to name but a few.

Harvesting: This seaweed takes some patience to harvest since it is so small, and often contains grit, other types of seaweed and little sea creatures that need to be picked out carefully. Although it is perennial, the best time to harvest it is from late winter to early spring since the quality will deteriorate throughout the summer. Cut it with a pair of sharp scissors holding a tub or bowl underneath to catch the fronds.

Taste: This seaweed has an intense salty, peppery, garlicky sea taste that chefs rave about and that has earned it the name 'truffle of the sea'. Usually sold and used in its dried form, it can be eaten fresh, too and pairs especially well with eggs, butter and shellfish (in much the same way that truffles do). The source of these flavours is terpenes, a group of molecules that protect the seaweed from grazing animals and that have a range of health benefits, although these are still not completely understood.

Nutritional highlights: The exact benefits of this seaweed have yet to be comprehensively researched and published.

Laver and nori

Laver has been used for centuries in coastal Wales, where it is best known as the main ingredient of laverbread, but *Porphyra* species have been around for much, much longer; their antiquity was recently confirmed by molecular studies that show that this species contains the most primitive plastid genome known to man. The Japanese have long been using their local species of *Porphyra*, too, although there it is known as nori. One of the most important seaweeds, its culinary use dates as far back as the 8th century CE and nowadays it mostly appears in the form of the dried and toasted square sheets that are wrapped around sushi rolls.

Also known as: Purple nori, slake, sloak, sloke, slabhac

Botanical name: *Porphyra* spp.

Colour: Olive-green to brown-purple or black, sometimes with green edges.

Description: Laver generally grows from a tiny discoid holdfast to about 30cm (12in) in length and is only one cell thin. About six species of nori are recognised but all are very similar in texture – membranous but tough. When it has been out of the water for a while it looks like an oil slick sticking on the rocks.

Habitat and distribution: Most often found in the lower to upper shore on sand-scoured boulders and rocks on the more exposed shores, it often grows mixed with gutweed. *Porphyra* species are highly adaptable, being capable of tolerating both great wave action and prolonged periods of exposure to the air, and it can grow singly or in dense colonies. Most common in spring and summer, it occurs around the UK where there is suitable habitat, as well as in the Faroe Islands; France; Helgoland; Ireland; Italy; Portugal; Spain and Iceland. The Japanese currently cultivate about 350,000 tonnes of nori a year, but the Chinese, Koreans and Vietnamese are quickly increasing their production levels as well.

Harvesting: Different species are available at different times of the year, generally (but not exclusively) on more exposed coasts. Cut halfway using scissors, taking only a small quantity here and there and making sure you don't damage the holdfast.

Taste: Laver/nori is mild in taste when fresh but stronger when dried. Toasted, it is at its most toothsome, having a nutty, moreish flavour. It is one of the few seaweeds that makes an excellent ingredient in sweet dishes, and in South Wales it is boiled and used to make a jelly.

Nutritional highlights: *Porphyra* contains the least iodine of all the seaweeds. It is especially high in zinc and vitamins A, B2, B9 and C, but it also contains a range of other vitamins and minerals.

Irish moss and grape pip weed

What is generally referred to as Irish moss actually covers two species, which are similar
in appearance and have the same properties. The main one is Irish moss, the other grape pip weed,
the reproductive structures of which resemble grape pips. Both have the same culinary usage.

Also known as: Carrageen, carrageenan, carrageen moss, carraigín, Dorset weed, pearl moss, sea pearl moss, jelly moss, rock moss, gristle moss, curly moss, curly gristle moss; and grape pip weed, false Irish moss, false carragheen, carraigínclúimhín cait

Botanical name: *Chondrus crispus* and *Mastocarpus stellatus*

Colour: Both types are dark brown to dark red with bushy cartilaginous fronds that resemble kale. The tips of the fronds are sometimes lime green. When underwater, *Chondrus crispus* can display an iridescent blue reflection.

Description: Small, between 10-22cm (4-9in) in length, both have flat fronds. Those of *Chondrus crispus* are thicker in the middle than at the edges, and branch out from a discoid holdfast, whereas *Mastocarpus stellatus* consists of strap-like blades with thickened margins that roll inwards on themselves to form a distinctive channel. They are easily identifiable by touch, since they have a wiry, bushy texture.

Habitat and distribution: Both types are found, often in large continuous mats, on rocks on the lower shores and in the shallow subtidal, or in rock pools in the mid-intertidal, while *Chondrus crispus* also occurs to a depth of about 24m (79ft). They occur in many areas of the UK (but not parts of the east coast) and Ireland – especially the western coasts – and can also be found widely in the north-western and north-eastern Atlantic. Similar, usable species are found in the colder waters of Pacific Russia, Japan, China and Korea, Pacific South America and the western coast of North America.

Harvesting: Irish moss and grape pip weed are available year round, but are at their best from late spring and through the summer. As usual, care should be taken and scissors should be used to cut the seaweed at least one-third of the way up from the holdfast. Both types emanate a pungent aroma if dried for storage in the house, so it is best to dry them outdoors for a few days on an old sheet or mat, if possible.

Taste: Irish moss and grape pipe weed are primarily used as thickening agents in the same way as gelatine, and are almost flavourless when bleached, apart from a faintly sweet aroma, which might add more depth to a dish. When used unbleached, the taste is stronger. If using lemon juice or another acidic ingredient in the dish, this should be added at the end of the cooking time or it might interfere with the thickening process.

Nutritional highlights: Irish moss has known anti-viral properties and also acts as an expectorant, which is why it is so widely used in cough medicines. Both species contain many trace elements, vitamins and minerals, and Irish moss is especially high in magnesium.

IS CARRAGEENAN SAFE?

The cell-wall substance in seaweeds such as Irish moss and grape pip weed that acts as a thickener and stabiliser is called carrageenan. It is widely used industrially and is found in a wide range of products including beer, ice cream, sauces, pet-food, toothpaste and shampoo. However this form of carrageenan is not the naturally occurring form. Instead it is processed by cooking it in hot alkali, and using isopropanol or potassium chloride, apparently changing the actual molecular structure.

Some studies have suggested that some forms of carrageenan, called poligeenan, may be harmful to our health. It is therefore advised that food-grade processed carrageenan should contain a minimal amount of the degraded form, poligeenan, and carrageenans sold by reputable manufacturers generally meet these standards. Carrageenan extracted by boiling whole Irish moss does not resemble the carrageenan obtained industrially and the health concerns and research associated do not apply to this.

Sea spaghetti

Sea spaghetti is quite unmistakable. With its long, smooth fronds it can carpet large areas of more sheltered rocky areas, where it grows explosively – a good job, since it is tasty and versatile, and becoming increasingly popular and more widely available in supermarkets.

Also known as: Thongweed, sea thong, sea haricots, buttonweed, ríseach

Botanical name: *Himanthalia elongata*

Colour: Yellow to yellow-green when young, becoming brown when older. Dark brown to black when dried.

Description: Some individuals can grow to more than 2m (6½ft) in length. The first year, a small mushroom-like button forms from which grow long strands that resemble tagliatelle or spaghetti. These easily recognisable fronds float to the surface of the water and are therefore easy to find.

Habitat and distribution: One of the more common species in the UK, sea spaghetti can be found on the lower shore, especially when it is semi-exposed to waves. It can cover extensive areas, forming dense mats through which swimming is not an option, and is only exposed at the lowest spring tides. Its distribution is limited to the eastern Atlantic, where it occurs in several regions in Europe, including Ireland; the Channel Islands; the Faroe Islands; north-west France; Helgoland; the Netherlands; Norway; and northern Portugal and Spain.

Harvesting: Sea spaghetti fronds start to appear from spring and die back in late autumn. Cut some of the fronds using scissors, taking care to leave the distinctive button-like holdfast intact on the rocks.

Taste: Sea spaghetti tastes like mildly salted asparagus when young and fresh, becoming stronger later in the season, but remaining a very mild-tasting seaweed. It adds a meaty flavour to stocks and soups, and young specimens can be served fresh in salads or pickled. The older it is, the tougher it becomes, in which instance it requires cooking. It is available fresh or dried.

Nutritional highlights: High in calcium, magnesium, zinc, iodine, and vitamins A, E, C, B1, B2, B7 and B9.

Kelp and kombu

A familiar sight in many places in the world, kelp forms undulating meadows of flexible golden-brown fronds along rocky shores at low tide. Not especially palatable given its tough texture, *Laminaria digitata* is primarily harvested for alginate production, although some is dried and eaten. Kombu, or *Saccharina japonica*, is the Pacific variety of kelp that is widely used in Asian kitchens, especially those in Japan and in particular Okinawa, and in other parts of the world, too.

Also known as: Kombu, oarweed, tangle, red ware, sea girdles, tangle tail, sea wand, sea ware, horsetail kelp, strap wrack, leath, learach

Botanical name: *Laminaria digitata* and *Saccharina japonica* (formerly called *Laminaria japonica*)

Colour: *Laminaria digitata* is brown when young, becoming darker brown when it is older. It is dark brown to dark green when dried. *Saccharina japonica* is dark green to dark brown and greyish black, the darker leaves commonly being considered better for consumption.

Description: Generally up to 2m (6½ft) long, *Laminaria digitata* has a smooth oval stipe that bends double without snapping. The slippery blade is often divided into separate fingers, something that is caused by wave action and explains its name. It can be confused with forest kelp (*Laminaria hyperborea*), which grows in deeper water and has a thicker, rough and round stipe that stays erect when out of the water (see page 53). *Saccharina japonica* has long, belt-shaped, broad fronds with wavy margins.

Habitat and distribution: *Laminaria digitata* is common around the UK apart from the south-east coast, and also occurs in the Arctic (Canada, Svalbard and the White Sea), and around the Atlantic Islands; in many parts of Europe, including the Channel Islands, Ireland, the Faroe Islands, Scandinavia, the Netherlands, France, Germany, Spain, Helgoland, Russia and Romania; as well as various areas of North America. *Saccharina japonica* can be found in Japan, Korea, China and the Pacific coast of Russia. The vast majority of kelp that is sold is farmed on ropes suspended from or emanating from floating rafts (see page 10), and kelp is the most important economic seaweed in China.

Harvesting: *Laminaria digitata* grows in the lower intertidal and shallow subtidal on rock, and is only exposed at low spring tides, when it can be harvested in the normal manner – with scissors, well above the intersection between the blade and the stipe in order to allow for future regrowth. Kelp is mostly produced and harvested commercially in the East. Both are at their best during the summer.

Taste: Kelp is not very palatable when eaten fresh from the ocean because it is tough and leathery but, once dried, it tastes liquorice-like, salty and subtly sweet. The Japanese use kelp, which has pronounced umami properties, as a flavour-enhancer in soups and broths where, together with bonito flakes, it forms the base for dashi. It can also be cut into strips and pickled, or used to wrap food, as well as for a tea. The surface of dried kelp is often covered with white deposits of mannitol (a naturally occurring sugar).

Nutritional highlights: Dried kelp is high in calcium, magnesium, iron, copper, potassium and zinc, and vitamins B7 and D. It is the food containing most iodine in the world (see also Iodine on page 18).

KELP IN COOKING

Kelp is not a single species of seaweed: it is the collective name for brown seaweeds in the Laminariales order. It can sometimes be used to describe the burning of any seaweed, mainly Laminaria and Fucus species, for the production of soda ash and potash. But in culinary terms and in this book kelp refers to the oarweed or kombu variety.

Sugar kelp

This seaweed gets its name from the white sugar (mannitol) that forms on its surface when it is dried, which gives it a sweet flavour. It is similar in taste to kelp and can be used in much the same way, but is easier to forage for than buy since it generally grows wild rather than being predominantly cultivated and controlled.

Also known as: Sea belt, sweet kombu, poor man's weatherglass, sweet wrack, sugar tang, sweet tangle, rufaí, ribíní, rufa

Botanical name: *Saccharina latissima* (formerly called *Laminaria saccharina*)

Colour: Brown in the middle, with lighter-brown or yellow-brown edges.

Description: Sugar kelp generally grows up to 3m (10ft) long from a claw-like holdfast that grips on to rocks, boulders and cobbles. It has a rather short stipe and a single continuous frond that reminds one of a conveyor belt with creased curly edges. It can be confused with Atlantic wakame (*Alaria esculenta*) but is identifiable for its lack of a midrib and the dimpled surface of its fronds.

Habitat and distribution: Sugar kelp grows on the extreme lower shore in very disturbed areas, occasionally in rock pools, and in sheltered spots with fast-flowing waters, such as rapids, down to a

depth of about 30m (98 feet). It can also be found growing on marina walls. This is an annual species that can only be found in the summer throughout the UK apart from in the south-east, and in Ireland. Elsewhere, it occurs in too many regions for them all to be listed here, but in brief it is found from northern Russia down to Spain and Portugal; around Greenland; along the Pacific coast of America down to New Jersey; in the Bering Straits; and in Japan.

Harvesting: Harvest during the summer in the UK; throughout the year elsewhere. Only cut off the top third of the frond, using sharp scissors or a knife.

Taste: Savoury sweet in flavour, sugar kelp is the most similar species in taste to the kelp used in dashi and miso soup.

Nutritional highlights: Like *Laminaria digitata* and *Saccharina japonica*, sugar kelp is high in calcium, magnesium, iron, copper, potassium and zinc, and vitamins B7 and D. It is also very high in iodine.

Atlantic wakame

This cold-water-loving seaweed is popular for its pleasant, mild flavour as well as its many health benefits. It is similar to Pacific wakame (see page 49), but being a little more fibrous it requires a longer cooking time.

Also known as: Alaria, wing kelp, murlins, dabberlocks, bladderlocks, edible kelp, honeyware, henware, stringy kelp, horsetail kelp, fruill, ribíní

Botanical name: *Alaria esculenta*

Colour: Dark brown or olive fronds with a distinctive lighter yellow-brown midrib.

Description: Measuring 1–1.5m (3¼–5ft) in length, sometimes more than 2m (6½ft), Atlantic wakame resembles a very long bird feather – indeed the Latin name translates as 'edible wings'. It has a root-like holdfast and a flexible narrow stipe, which carries on along the frond as a distinct midrib that clearly marks it out from other species, apart from its invasive Asian counterpart, Pacific wakame.

Habitat and distribution: Atlantic wakame grows along very exposed rocky shores with lots of wave action, and also in the lower shore in tidal pools. It prefers cold water, which is why it degenerates in the summer, especially in the south of the UK, where waters may become too warm. It occurs along many western shores of the UK, and in the north-east, as well as around Ireland and the Scottish islands. Elsewhere, it grows in the many regions found in the North Atlantic as far south as Brittany in France and the Bering Strait; in the Bering Sea; and in the Sea of Japan.

Harvesting: Harvest from early to late spring, while the water is still cold enough. Only harvest the top third of the front with sharp scissors or a knife.

Taste: Very tasty and palatable, Atlantic wakame is sweetish and mild, similar to Pacific wakame. The fresh type can be toasted to make 'crisps', or marinated, blanched or steamed and used in salads and soups. It can also be dried and powdered and used to fortify drinks, or for an instant mineral-rich broth with the addition of some hot water.

Nutritional highlights: Atlantic wakame is high in calcium, magnesium, iron, potassium and trace elements, B vitamins, vitamin A (beta-carotene) and fibre.

Bladderwrack

Commonly used in thalassotherapy and cosmetics, bladderwrack also has a place in the kitchen. It is abundant and long-lived, sometimes surviving for up to five years, and can grow to impressive lengths in sheltered spots, coating rocks in slippery strands that may pop under your feet as you clamber around.

Also known as: Lady wrack, sea ware, sea wrack, rockweed, bladder fucus, black tang, fucus

Botanical name: *Fucus vesiculosus*

Colour: Olive green/brown

Description: This seaweed is part of the wrack family and resembles egg wrack and, in particular, serrated wrack. It differs from the latter in that it has smooth edges and air bladders that are usually in pairs on either side of the prominent midrib. It has a short stipe and a round holdfast. A form without the bladders occurs in wave-exposed shores.

Habitat and distribution: Common and abundant in the mid-intertidal of rocky shores in more sheltered areas throughout the UK, bladderwrack can withstand a range of exposures. It also occurs in the Faroes; the Baltic Sea; Norway; Sweden; Denmark; Germany; the Netherlands; Belgium; the Atlantic coast of Spain, France and Morocco; Madeira; and the eastern shores of Canada and the USA.

Harvesting: You can forage for bladderwrack throughout the year, although it contains its highest levels of vitamin A in the summer, and vitamin C in the autumn. Pick only a few fronds from each plant, cutting them well away from the stipe and holdfast.

Taste: It is best used when dried and ground, then sprinkled into food such as pasta dishes, in which case it tastes a little bit like Parmesan cheese. The tips can also be marinated and steamed, or used for stock or a flavour base for cooking fish, since their delicate flavour will complement rather than compete with other ingredients.

Nutritional highlights: It contains a wide range of minerals, vitamins and trace elements, especially vitamins A and C, and has antiviral properties.

OTHER TYPES OF WRACK

Serrated wrack (Fucus serratus) *deserves a mention, even though this species is by no means one of the tastier seaweeds and eating it is not recommended. However, it is very good for the skin since the gel it produces has moisturising, anti-microbial and soothing properties. It can thus be used in the bath or as a poultice, and it is one of the main seaweeds used in thalassotherapy, a hot seaweed-infused bath that is popular in France.*

Serrated wrack is very similar to bladderwrack in appearance, although it lacks the bladders and its fronds have serrated, saw-toothed fringes. It grows in the lower shore, intermixed with kelp and Irish moss, and is very common around the UK and from Spain northwards to Spitsbergen.

Egg wrack (Ascophyllum nodosum) *is not the most palatable of the wracks and its uses are mainly limited to fertiliser, livestock feed and alginate extraction. The main egg-wrack producers are Scotland, Ireland, Iceland and Norway. It is also known as yellow tang, knotted wrack, asco, sea whistle, rockweed, Norwegian kelp and knotted kelp.*

Olive green/brown in colour, egg wrack is part of the Fucus family and is a little similar to bladderwrack and serrated wrack. It differs from these in that it is greener in colour, and instead of having a midrib and leafy side parts it is a broad ribbon with branches that produce single large egg-like bladders. It is common and abundant in the mid-intertidal throughout the UK and is generally confined to the North Atlantic basin.

OTHER IMPORTANT SEAWEEDS

There are a few other seaweeds that are worth a mention because they are important economically around the world, and some of which are edible. Where they do not occur locally, they may be available to buy in dried form.

VELVET HORN

Velvet horn (*Codium* species) is mostly eaten in the Far East and has long been used in Chinese medicine as a vermifuge (a treatment for parasitic worms and other internal parasites) and to treat urinary disease.

Also known as spongeweed, green sea fingers, dead man's fingers, green fleece, oyster thief and sponge tang, this pale to dark moss-green seaweed is quite unmistakable due to its bush-like appearance, fleshy fronds emanating from a disc-shaped holdfast, and velvety smooth texture when the fronds are submerged. Once washed ashore or dried, the fronds lose their hairs and feel coarse to the touch.

There are two types of velvet horn in the UK (there are more elsewhere in the world): the native *Codium tomentosum*, which reaches 25cm (10in) in length and is distinctly flattened where the fronds branch; and its invasive cousin, *Codium fragile*, which is larger, is not flattened at the forks, and has pointed frond tips. The latter type seems to be outcompeting the UK's native species, which is now very uncommon and declining.

Where it is available, velvet horn is available throughout the year, but especially in spring and autumn. It can be found in rock pools and rocks in the lower shore and also washed up on beaches. It is mainly located in the south-west of the UK, and in Ireland; northern France; northern Spain; the Netherlands; the Azores; the Adriatic coast of Italy; Greece; Australia and New Zealand; and North America. When harvesting, cut up to half of the plant, leaving enough to grow back. Make sure to remove any snails and wash it well.

In culinary terms, it has an earthy flavour that is reminiscent of oysters and should be eaten raw, since it disintegrates once cooked. In Hawaii it is eaten raw with tomatoes in salads, and in Japan it is preserved in salt. It is high in protein, beta-carotene, sodium, iron, sulphur, iodine, calcium, magnesium, phosphorus and potassium and vitamins C and E.

PACIFIC WAKAME

Pacific wakame (*Undaria pinnatifida*) is considered to be among the worst 100 invasive species in the world by the International Union for the Conservation of Nature (IUCN). Its collection is prohibited without a special licence to avoid its inadvertent spread, but it is cultivated and collected under licence for consumption in its native home in the cold waters around Japan, China and Korea. Elsewhere, it is established in a range of other countries, including New Zealand, the USA, France, the UK, Spain, Italy, Argentina, Australia and Mexico, having travelled as hull fouling on ships from Asia and in Europe as a contaminant of Pacific oyster spat. It grows in the lower intertidal and very shallow subtidal in sheltered locations such as harbours, and especially on structures such as buoys, marina walls and on boat hulls.

In terms of appearance, Pacific wakame is yellowish to dark brown in colour, and similar to Atlantic wakame in that it has the same midrib, although the stipe is more wavy and corrugated and the frond has pronounced indents. It normally grows to 1–2m (3½–6½ft) in length and has a claw-like holdfast.

In the kitchen, it is easy to see why Pacific wakame is so popular in Asia, since it has a subtle sweet-and-salty taste and a soft texture that makes it an ideal ingredient in the ever-popular soups and salads. It also has many health benefits, and is particularly notable for its levels of fucoidan – a compound that has anti-viral properties and may have anti-tumour benefits – as well as being a good source of calcium, iodine, iron, magnesium, folate, and vitamins A, C, D, E, K and B2.

JAPANESE WIREWEED

Japanese wireweed (*Sargassum muticum*), as the name implies, is Japanese in origin. Like Pacific wakame, it is thought to owe its now global distribution to imported Japanese oysters, with which it hitches a ride. It is a particular nuisance because it can form large, dense floating mats that clog up harbours, get stuck in boat props and fishing lines, and trap plastic. It owes these characteristics to its rapid growth rate and because it can reproduce vegetatively. Since this is an invasive species the whole plant should be removed when harvesting, making sure no parts break off, disperse and continue to grow.

Wireweed is used as fertiliser, fish feed, as a thickening agent and as a medicine. Its taste is quite bitter, so it is not terribly suitable for the kitchen.

HIJIKI

Hijiki (*Sargassum fusiforme*) is a brown seaweed found in Japan, Korea and China. It is an important seaweed in the diet of the Japanese, where it is cooked and dried before being sold both locally and abroad. Lately, however, the Food Standards Agency has advised people not to eat hijiki since it contains high levels of inorganic arsenic.

ARAME

Arame (*Ecklonia bicyclis*) is another important commercial edible seaweed. It is mainly found in the waters around Japan, but is now cultivated in different areas, too, such as South Korea. It has a mild, semi-sweet flavour, and a delicate but firm texture, making it a very versatile seaweed for use in sweet and savoury dishes. It is usually sold in dried strips.

GRACILARIA

There are different species of the genus Gracilaria, which are all fairly similar to each other and are therefore easily confused. A few species are present in the UK, the most common one being slender wart weed (*Gracilaria gracilis*). Gracilarias are relatively small red seaweeds that may resemble a branchy moss and are rather cartilaginous. They are commercially important seaweeds that are cultivated in India, Japan, Argentina, Hawaii, Sweden, the USA and many other countries, mostly to produce agar.

Left: Japanese wireweed (*Sargassum muticum*).
Opposite, top left: Hijiki (*Sargassum fusiforme*).
Opposite, top right: Arame (*Ecklonia bicyclis*).
Opposite bottom: *Gracilaria gracilis.*

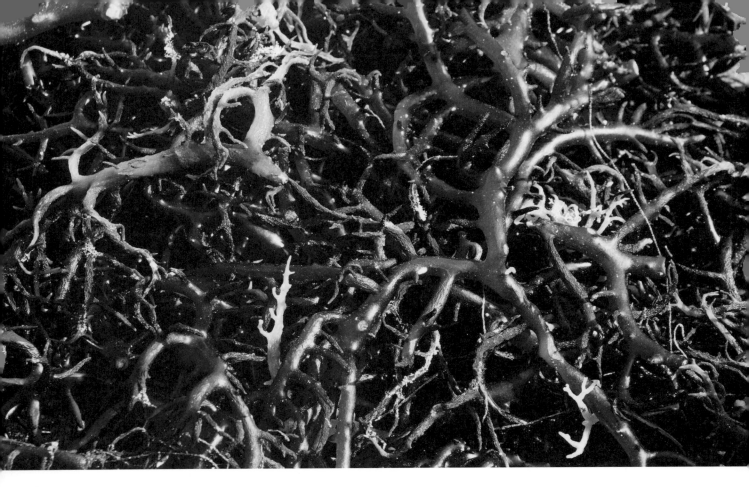

EUCHEUMA

Eucheuma cottonii is an industry name for *Kappaphycus alvarezii*. It is grown by aquaculture mainly in the Philippines, Indonesia, Tanzania and Brazil for carrageenan production. About 65,000 tonnes of carrageenan are now used by the food and other industries.

SEA GRAPES

Sea grapes (*Caulerpa lentillifera*) is a green warm-water species of seaweed. Its small bladders are succulent and resemble caviar in appearance and taste. It is cultivated in South-east Asia and recently also on a very small scale in the Netherlands.

FOREST KELP

Forest kelp (*Laminaria hyperborea*) is a relative of kelp. It is a very important seaweed since it forms extensive underwater forests around the world that we rely upon for wave dissipation, prevention of erosion, oxygen supply, CO_2 capture, and to combat ocean acidification. Moreover, the forests are home to a large variety of marine species including fish, crabs, lobsters, other seaweeds and many invertebrates, a fact that assists fisheries and helps to maintain fish stocks. Once cast ashore after a storm, forest kelp also forms an important habitat for many small creatures that in turn are food for birds, crabs and other species.

In terms of appearance, forest kelp closely resembles kelp or oarweed, but differs by having a stipe that remains rigid when out of the water. The stipe is also rough and round instead of being smooth and oval. The fronds are usually thicker, more leathery, lighter in colour and shorter.

Forest kelp is not used in the kitchen. Its main use is as a source of alginates for thickening agents in the food, medicine and cosmetics industries. In France, it is harvested on a large scale using boats carrying Scoubidou – big rotating combs that rip up the seaweed.

BULL KELP

Bull kelp or bullwhip kelp (*Nereocystis luetkeana*) is the Northern Pacific equivalent of the forest kelp (*Laminaria hyperborea*) that is found in the North Atlantic, and has similar benefits and uses. It is a large brown seaweed that has a single bladder at the top of the stipe that is filled with nitrogen, oxygen and carbon monoxide, which helps it to float to upwards from its holdfast. Together with giant kelp it forms huge kelp forests that stretch from California to Alaska.

GIANT KELP

Giant kelp (*Macrocystis pyrifera*) is the largest seaweed in the world. It occurs on the north-east coast of the Pacific together with bull kelp and is also found in the colder areas of South America, South Africa and Australia. It can reach over 45m (148ft) in length in just one season and can grow up to 60cm (24in) per day.

Opposite top: Eucheuma cottonii (*Kappaphycus alvarezii*).
Opposite bottom: Sea grapes (*Caulerpa lentillifera*).
Above right: Bull kelp (*Nereocystis luetkeana*).
Right: Giant kelp (*Macrocystis pyrifera*).

SEAWEEDY PLANTS

There are a few common species that you might encounter in and around the ocean that are often confused as being seaweeds, but are in fact flowering plants, not algae. Many have culinary or other uses.

EELGRASS

Eelgrass (*Zostera marina*), very much looks like you would expect grass to appear. Even though it is a widespread species, with different varieties growing around the world, you are unlikely to see it on dry land because it grows below the tidal zone in sheltered areas in sandy and muddy places such as estuaries, sandy beaches, bays and lagoons. It is used as a food by the Seri tribe in Mexico. Only the rhizomes (the part of the stem of the plant that grows horizontally in the soil and from where new shoots can grow) and the blade bases of the plant are eaten - fresh or dried. In some countries the dried blades have been used to insulate houses, thatch roofs, as fertiliser and feedstock, and even to stuff mattresses.

MARSH SAMPHIRE

Marsh samphire (from the French Saint Pierre) - also called salicornia, sampkin, sea asparagus or sampha and the Latin name of which is *Salicornia europaea* - is often mistaken for a seaweed, but is in fact a flowering plant that likes to get its feet wet and salty. It grows around estuaries and tidal creeks and prefers things to be muddy. The keen observer might notice three things that distinguish it from seaweeds: it grows higher up the beach; it grows in muddy areas instead of clinging to rocks; and it has tiny flowers. Marsh samphire has a mild, lightly salty and very agreeable taste, making it a chef's favourite.

ROCK SAMPHIRE

It is immediately obvious that rock samphire (*Crithmum maritimum*) is not a seaweed. It usually grows quite far from the reaches of the sea on higher (and often steep) cliffs and its yellow-white flowers are another give-away sign it is not a seaweed. It has a strong lemony smell and flavour.

SEA PURSLANE

Found in salt marshes around the coast of England and Wales, sea purslane (*Atriplex portulacoides*) is very robust, withstanding conditions that few other species can tolerate, and indeed thriving in many estuaries and mud flats in these regions. Silvery in appearance thanks to the tiny papery scales that coat the short, thick, oval leaves, it is at its best in spring and summer (although it is available year round) and can be used sparingly in salads or, more commonly, as a seasoning, to replace salt.

Opposite left: Eelgrass (*Zostera marina*).
Opposite right: Marsh samphire (*Salicornia europaea*).
Above: Rock samphire (*Crithmum maritimum*).

TABLE OF COMMON SEAWEEDS

Name	What it looks like	Regions in which it is found	Where on the shoreline it is found
Sea lettuce (*Ulva lactuca*)		Most places worldwide, especially Europe; North America; Central America; the Caribbean Islands; South America; Africa; Indian Ocean Islands; Pacific Islands; China; South-west Asia; Australia and New Zealand	On rock, in rock pools in the lower shore, and in the shallow subtidal
Gutweed (*Ulva intestinalis*)		Most places worldwide, especially in the Baltic and Mediterranean Seas and the Pacific Ocean, and waters around the Azores; Belgium; Denmark; Ireland; Norway; Poland; Russia; Alaska; the Aleutian Islands; Puget Sound; Japan; Korea; Mexico; the Philippines and Israel	Rock pools in the upper intertidal, and salt marshes
Velvet horn (*Codium fragile*)		South-west of the UK, and in Ireland; northern France; northern Spain; the Netherlands; the Azores; the Adriatic coast of Italy; Greece; Australia and New Zealand; and North America	Rock pools and rocks in the lower shore, and washed up on beaches
Dulse (*Palmaria palmata*)		The UK; and from Arctic Russia to Portugal; the Baltic; Arctic Canada to New Jersey (USA); also perhaps in Japan and Korea, though this has not been verified as being the same species	The intertidal and subtidal zones; on the stipes of forest kelp; on mussels
Pepper dulse (*Osmundea pinnatifida*)		Throughout the UK apart from in the south-east, as well as in parts of Ireland and the Channel Islands. Many other regions, including: non-Mediterranean areas of Europe; several Atlantic Islands; tropical and subtropical western Atlantic; the USA (Florida and North Carolina); temperate South America; a few parts of Africa; Cyprus; Turkey; Yemen; Pakistan; India; Korea; Taiwan; Indonesia and the Philippines	On open rock surfaces in the middle and lower intertidal, and the subtidal
Laver and nori (*Porphyra sp.*)		Laver grows around the UK where there is suitable habitat; as well as in the Faroe Islands; France; Helgoland; Ireland; Italy; Portugal; Spain and Iceland. Nori is intensively cultivated in Japan, Vietnam and China	Lower to upper shore on sand-scoured boulders and rocks on the more exposed shores
Irish moss and grape pip weed (*Chondrus crispus* and *Mastocarpus stellatus*)		Many parts of the UK and Ireland; widely in the north-western and north-eastern Atlantic; as well regions ranging from Taiwan, Japan, Ghana and Angola to Iceland, many parts of North America, the Falkland Islands and many European countries	Both occur on rocks on the lower shores and in the shallow subtidal, or in rock pools in the mid-intertidal; *Chondrus crispus* also occurs to a depth of about 24m (79ft)

When to harvest	How to harvest	Nutritional benefits	Uses
All year, but best in late spring and summer	Cut the frond halfway, leaving behind the holdfast and some of the frond	Calcium, copper, iodine, iron, magnesium, manganese, potassium and zinc, and vitamins A, C, E, B2, B9 and B12	Commonly used in soups and salads, or dried and flaked and used as a seasoning
All year, but best in late spring and summer	Cut the frond halfway, leaving behind the holdfast and some of the frond	Calcium, copper, iodine, iron, magnesium, manganese, potassium and zinc, and vitamins A, C, E, B2, B9 and B12	Very similar to sea lettuce, it can be used in soups and salads, or dried and flaked and employed as a seasoning
Year round	Cut part of each individual and leave some branches behind	Protein, beta-carotene, sodium, iron, sulphur, iodine, calcium, magnesium, phosphorus and potassium, and vitamins C and E	Eaten raw in salads, or preserved in salt; should not be cooked
All year, but at its best in spring	Cut part of each individual and leave some branches behind	High in calcium, iron, iodine, copper, manganese, magnesium, potassium and zinc and in vitamins A, B1, B2, B9, B12 and C	Can be eaten raw in salads or added to other dishes, but is generally sold in its dried form
Late winter to early spring	Cut part of each individual and leave some branches behind	The exact benefits of this seaweed have yet to be comprehensively researched and published	Usually sold in its dried form, but can be used fresh
Different species are available at different times of the year, meaning one species or another is usually available	Cut only part of each frond to allow regrowth	Vitamins A, B2, B9 and C, and zinc, as well as a wide range of other vitamins and minerals	Suitable for use fresh or dried, its mild taste when fresh makes it suitable for use in desserts
Year round, but best from late spring to early autumn	Remove just a few branches, leaving behind the holdfast and some fronds	Many trace elements, vitamins and minerals; especially high in magnesium	Both are primarily used as thickening agents in the same way as gelatine

Name	What it looks like	Regions in which it is found	Where on the shoreline it is found
Sea spaghetti (*Himanthalia elongata*)		Very common in the UK; also found in many regions in Europe, including Ireland; the Channel Islands; the Faroe Islands; north-west France; Helgoland; the Netherlands; Norway; and northern Portugal and Spain	On the lower shore, especially when it is semi-exposed to waves
Kelp and kombu (*Laminaria digitata* and *Saccharina japonica*)		*Laminaria digitata* is common around the UK (apart from along the south-east coast); Canada, Svalbard, the White Sea and the Atlantic Islands; in many parts of Europe, including Ireland, the Channel Islands, the Faroe Islands, Scandinavia, the Netherlands, France, Germany, Spain, Helgoland, Russia and Romania; and various areas of North America. *Saccharina japonica* can be found in Japan, Korea, China and the Pacific coast of Russia	*Laminaria digitata* grows in the lower intertidal and shallow subtidal on rock. *Saccharina japonica* is mostly grown on ropes
Sugar kelp (*Saccharina latissima*)		Around the UK apart from in the south-east, and in Ireland. It occurs in too many regions to be listed here, from northern Russia down to Spain and Portugal; around Greenland; along the Pacific coast of America down to New Jersey; in the Bering Straits; and in Japan	On the extreme lower shore in very disturbed areas; occasionally in rock pools; and in sheltered spots with fast-flowing waters
Atlantic wakame (*Alaria esculenta*)		Many western shores of the UK, and in the north-east; around Ireland and the Scottish islands; many regions in the North Atlantic as far south as Brittany in France and the Bering Strait; in the Bering Sea; and in the Sea of Japan	Along very exposed rocky shores with lots of wave action, and also in the lower shore in tidal pools
Pacific wakame (*Undaria pinnatifida*)		Considered to be among the worst 100 invasive species in the world by the International Union for the Conservation of Nature (IUCN). It originated in the cold waters of Japan, Korea and China, but is now established in a range of other countries, including the UK, New Zealand, the USA, France, Spain, Italy, Argentina, Australia and Mexico	Lower intertidal and very shallow subtidal in sheltered locations
Bladderwrack (*Fucus vesiculosus*)		Common throughout the UK, as well as the Faroes; the Baltic Sea; Norway; Sweden; Denmark; Germany; the Netherlands; Belgium; the Atlantic coast of Spain, France and Morocco; Madeira; and the eastern shores of Canada and the USA	Mid-intertidal of rocky shores in more sheltered areas

When to harvest	How to harvest	Nutritional benefits	Uses
Spring to summer	Cut some of the fronds using scissors, taking care to leave the distinctive button-like holdfasts intact on the rocks	High in calcium, magnesium, zinc, iodine, and vitamins A, E, C, B1, B2, B7 and B9	A mild-tasting seaweed that can be bought both fresh or dried, and used in a wide range of dishes
Best in summer	Cut well above the intersection between blade and stipe, to allow new growth	High in calcium, magnesium, iron, copper, potassium and zinc, and vitamins B7 and D. It contains more iodine than any other food, so care must be taken not to exceed recommended safe levels	The umami qualities of these seaweeds make them very popular, and they are most commonly used in their dried form, notably in dashi
Summer	Cut fronds well above the stipe to allow regrowth	High in calcium, magnesium, iron, copper, potassium and zinc, and vitamins B7 and D. It is also very high in iodine	Similar to kelp, it can be used in soups and broths or as a flavour-enhancer in other foods, too
Early to late spring	Leave 20cm (8in) of blade attached to the rock	High in calcium, magnesium, iron, potassium and trace elements, B vitamins, vitamin A (beta-carotene) and fibre	Fresh wakame can be toasted, or marinated, blanched or steamed and used in salads and soups. It can also be dried and powdered
Harvesting must only be done under licence	Harvesting must only be done under licence	A good source of omega-3 fatty acids, calcium, iodine, iron, magnesium, folate, and vitamins A, C, D, E, K and B2. High in fucoidan, which is thought to have many beneficial properties	A key source of food in Japan, Korea and China, wakame is used in many dishes, such as soups – especially miso – and some salads
Year round, but contains its highest levels of vitamin A in the summer, and vitamin C in the autumn	Remove only a few fronds from each, cutting well away from the stipe and holdfast	A wide range of minerals, vitamins and trace elements, especially vitamins A and C, and has antiviral properties	Fresh tips can be marinated and steamed; more commonly used in its dried and ground form in cooking

FORAGING FOR SEAWEEDS

With the relevant permission, everyone can forage for seaweeds. Unlike mushrooms, virtually all seaweeds are edible (although not all of them are equally tasty) so you do not need to worry about poisoning yourself. One thing you do have to take into account, however, is the location, as seaweed can take up pollution. Try to avoid picking it near towns, places where there is run-off from farms, sewage outlets, harbours, or in other industrial areas. Sea lettuce and gutweed favour nutrient-rich waters, which could be an indication of polluted streams and sewage, and contamination of the seaweed.

Safe foraging

The seashore can be a dangerous place, so it is important to follow a few basic safety rules before and whilst foraging:

- *You should always tell someone exactly where you are going and when you expect to be back, and let them know when you have returned safely.*

- *Ensure you have with you a fully charged mobile phone and save on it emergency telephone numbers.*

- *Growing locations are often in very remote areas so it is advised to go in a pair or with a group.*

- *The young, weak or non-swimmers, and those with very little experience of the sea should always go with someone who knows what they are doing.*

- *Weather conditions are critical – avoid going out in heavy rain, high winds, when a storm is predicted, or cold.*

- *In some locations, the tide can come in quickly. It is not much fun to find yourself wading through waist-high water on the only way back after a good harvest, where less than an hour ago there was still solid rock. It therefore pays to carry a tide book, and be aware of the tidal movements in your area. These are usually available online, so check before you plan an expedition.*

- *Rocks, especially those covered with seaweed or that are wet, can be slippery so proceed with caution and wear suitable footwear. It is also advisable to wear hi-visibility clothing so that you can easily be spotted should you have an accident and require rescuing.*

Do not eat the seaweed that you can find lying on beaches at the high-tide mark. This seaweed has often been dead for a while and is probably decomposing nicely, fit only for becoming compost for your garden. The smell should give you enough warning! Seaweeds for eating are picked when they are alive.

It is important to consider that seaweed harvested in the UK and sold commercially has been tested for both microbiological activity (salmonella, E. coli etc) and heavy metals (such as arsenic) in approved laboratories under Food Standards regulations. Unless tested it is impossible to know what the seaweeds hold. Washing thoroughly and hand cutting from clean waters away from farms and towns and not during or after heavy rains is important and will help to reduce risks.

Rules and sustainability

To forage for seaweed for private or commercial purposes, you will need to have consent from the landowner. In the UK, both the intertidal and subtidal are owned by a range of institutions or private landowners and it can be a bit tricky to find out who owns which part of the shoreline. In Ireland, the rules of foraging for seaweed are set to change, becoming stricter as commercial collection is intensifying. Rules will vary globally, and may change, so it is very important to check with the relevant local authority before you set out.

In practice, if you forage seaweed for personal use and in very limited quantities using techniques that do not cause any damage to the ecosystem or impact on the species you are foraging, it seems unlikely that anyone would not allow you to go ahead. You could still potentially be accused of trespassing, but if you harvest just a small amount it is unlikely that theft will be added to your list of transgressions.

The key principle when harvesting is to do it sustainably. Allowing the targeted seaweed to regrow and avoiding damaging other seaweeds and sea creatures enables the ecosystem to provide its bounty for future years and generations. With this in mind, there are a few basic rules that will assure you can return often to the same stretch of coast without finding it devoid of life (see page 64).

Opposite top: It is best to go foraging with at least one other person.
Opposite left: Only harvest as much seaweed as you need, and take care not to clear-cut one particular area.
Opposite right: Be aware of wildlife, taking care not to step on any as well as avoiding picking seaweed bearing animals or their eggs.

Where and when to forage

As with any foraged product, the best time to pick seaweeds varies according to species. While some can be gathered throughout the year, others are only visible or big enough to harvest at certain times.

Although seaweeds can be found in all the world's oceans, they do not occur everywhere. Like plants, they derive their energy from sunlight, so they can only grow in waters where there is enough light. In addition, seaweeds need to be anchored to the seabed, or they will quickly be washed away. In practice this means that you will not find them on sandy or pebbly beaches. Instead, seaweeds feel most at home on rocky shores, and more so in areas that are fairly sheltered and have clear waters. Luckily, these can be found aplenty in the UK, although most species will be absent from the east coast around the North Sea area.

The name is a bit of a give-away: seaweeds live in the sea. It may seem as though this makes them a bit more difficult to pick, especially if you do not enjoy getting wet but, fortunately, staying dry is certainly an option. Around low tide, which happens twice every 24 hours, the seaweeds growing nearest the high-tide mark become exposed. Extremely low tides expose even more seaweed to the air and this is a prime time to go foraging.

You can find seaweeds exposed from about 1–2 hours before a spring low tide, which gives you enough time to pick the best seaweeds without getting your feet wet. It is during the extreme spring tides that occur around the equinoxes in March and September that you can also find some of the species that are generally submerged, such as kelp and sea spaghetti.

Tides

Tides are one of the main variables that determine when you can harvest seaweeds from the shore. A basic knowledge of the tides is therefore a must.

Tides are created by the combined gravitational forces of the Sun and the Moon. Gravitational pull increases with mass, and although the Sun has vastly more mass than the Moon, it is also almost 400 times further away. As a result, the Moon has a considerably greater influence than the Sun.

The part of the Earth that is nearest to the Moon will experience the greatest pull and this will cause the water to move towards it,

Opposite: You don't have to get soaked in order to collect seaweed, since many types are exposed at low tide and can be gathered from the rocks.
Above, right: This diagram illustrates how the relative positions of the Sun and the Moon have an impact on the tides; when the two align, the combined gravitational pull causes a spring tide, but when they are at right angles to each other the effect is lessened and there is a neap tide.

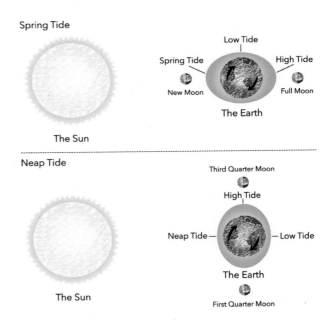

creating a large bulge or high tide. This also happens on the opposite side of the Earth. The areas at 90 degrees to these locations will, conversely, experience a low tide as the water is pulled away from it. As the Earth revolves once around its own axis every 24 hours, it will experience each bulge every day, resulting in (generally) two high tides a day.

However, the Moon does not stay still – it also revolves around the Earth, taking about 29 days and 12 hours to complete this cycle. So in the same 24 hours the Earth took to turn completely around its axis, the Moon moved a bit further as well. In fact, it takes the Moon about 24 hours and 50 minutes to be in the same spot in the sky, that is about 50 minutes later than the previous day. This is why with each successive day, high and low tides happen about 50 minutes later.

As mentioned, the Sun's forces also create those bulges, although they are considerably smaller. When the Moon and the Sun are aligned, however, their gravitational pulls are combined and this causes extremely high and low tides, which are called spring tides. When the Sun and Moon are at right angles to each other, the bulges cancel each other out to a certain degree, causing the smallest difference in tides. These are called neap tides.

Spring and neap tides happen twice a month: springs when the Sun and the Moon are on the same side of the Earth (new Moon) and when they are on opposite sides to each other (full Moon); neaps when they are at right angles (half Moon). The best time to go seaweed harvesting is therefore around spring low tides, when most seaweed is exposed to the air.

Cutting methods

Seaweed-picking should be a sustainable activity that does not damage the ecosystem. Doing it correctly is a vital part of ensuring that regrowth occurs. See page 60 for a few rules. How you cut the seaweed is especially important, and must always be done well above the area of growth or the seaweed will not be able to grow back again.

In the kelps, there is a specific area located at the beginning of the frond, where the stipe ends. Cut at least 5cm (2in) above this and only remove a few 'fingers' of each plant.

Sea spaghetti is one of the few species in which the meristem is located in the tips of the frond. Cutting it stops that frond from growing further. For this reason, it is best practice to cut off only a few fronds from each plant, leaving some behind to develop further. If you cut off all the fronds, no more will grow and the seaweed will simply die, which is unsustainable and may severely alter the regrowth for the following season.

In contrast, many other types of seaweed do not have a specific meristem or growth point. Dulse and sea lettuce, for instance, can be cut to about half to one-third of their natural size and new growth will appear soon after.

It is also important to harvest at the correct time of year for the seaweed species. Harvesting when the seaweeds are still very small and just starting to grow will often result in a larger proportion of the seaweed being taken than intended. This not only affects the amount that they will spore but also reduces the habitat for other creatures in the ecosystem. For example sea spaghetti starts to grow in springtime and is only a few centimetres for several weeks. Within a few months however it will be over a metre in length, and much more worthwhile to harvest.

Cutting rules

- Always leave the holdfast intact. When a seaweed is dislodged it will generally die. Avoid cutting too near the meristem – the place from which seaweeds grow. When this is cut off, the plant will die.
- Harvest sparsely and avoid clear-cutting.
- Avoid trampling on sensitive species.
- Cut each individual with scissors or a sharp knife.
- Avoid picking any seaweeds containing or bearing other species or their eggs, such as brittle stars, stalked jellyfish or sea hares.

Foraging gear

Not much equipment or specialist gear is needed to harvest seaweed. A sharp pair of scissors or knife, a basket or a suitable bag and a pair of wellington boots, galoshes or non-slip waterproof shoes will do the job nicely. If you do not want to wait for low spring tides and don't mind getting your feet and other body parts wet, nobody would stop you from jumping in with a snorkel and mask! When deciding what to wear on your feet, bear in mind that some walking will probably be involved and the fact that your footwear will possibly get a bit wet.

Above: Wear non-slip shoes when clambering on rocks.
Opposite, top: Sharp scissors and a bucket are all you really need to forage.
Opposite, left: Waterproof boots with grip soles are essential footwear.
Opposite, right: The meristem or growing point occurs in different places in different seaweed species, so take the time to learn where you should cut.

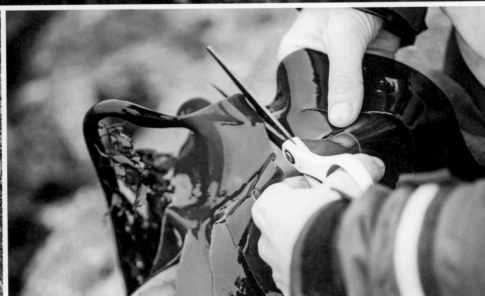

HOW TO TREAT FRESH SEAWEED

Having taken the trouble to harvest fresh seaweed, it needs to be cleaned and stored in an appropriate way so it can be useful as an ingredient. In order to prolong its shelf-life beyond the few days that fresh seaweed will keep in the refrigerator, it should be dried or frozen, and perhaps ground or flaked, depending upon the type and how you intend to use it.

Cleaning and soaking

Before eating or drying newly picked seaweed, it is a good idea to first quickly rinse it under the tap or in clean seawater. This will remove any sand and hiding sea life, such as shells and isopods, which can be remarkably well camouflaged and more numerous and frequently found in seaweed than you would perhaps think (see page 17). Don't worry too much though if you do discover a few at a later stage; these invertebrates are not poisonous or harmful. In fact, dried isopods taste remarkably like shrimp!

To avoid a loss of taste and the leaching of nutrients it is best not to soak seaweed for too long in fresh water. However, if you find the taste too strong, soaking will remove some of the salt. This is especially recommended for kelp, which contains high levels of iodine – about 20 minutes in cold water will reduce this to a more moderate, palatable level.

Drying

Seaweeds can be eaten raw, straight after picking and rinsing, but it is worth drying at least some of your haul so you have a stash for later. The easiest way to preserve seaweeds is to dry them. This will give it a shelf life of well over a year when done properly. The best means of doing this is to spread out the seaweed on the rocks where you picked them (bearing tides in mind, of course). This method has the benefit of greatly reducing the weight of the haul, making it easier to transport it back across the rocks and up the cliff.

Other options include in the sun in a garden, in a low oven, or with a heater or a dehumidifier. Whichever you use, the lower the temperature at which the seaweeds are dried, the more nutrients will be preserved. So, try to avoid temperatures above 50°C (122°F) – aim for about 40°C (104°F). Dried seaweed can lose 90 per cent of its mass when dried thoroughly, although this varies according to species, making it much more compact to store.

When drying seaweed at home, small species can be laid out on a tray or another clean surface, such as a plastic sheet. Make sure you spread them out well – don't lay them out too thickly as this will increase the drying time. Bigger species such as kelp, sea spaghetti and sugar kelp are best dried hanging out on a washing line. It may be necessary to bring these back inside at the end of the day and to store them in an airtight plastic container for the night. Seaweeds love moisture, and they will quickly soak up all the night-time and morning dew.

Powdering and flaking

When the seaweed is dried and feels crispy, virtually all of the water content will have gone. At this point it is worth grinding the seaweed to flakes or a powder, if desired, since over time the dried seaweed in its whole form will always absorb at least a little moisture from the air, making flaking or powdering at a later stage more difficult.

The best way is to grind the seaweed using a pestle and mortar, or in a blender, until the desired flake size or powder consistency is achieved. When using a blender, do not overfill the machine since this stops it from operating effectively and might cause it to overheat.

Seaweed overheating during the flaking process has been one of the hardest challenges to overcome for us at The Cornish Seaweed Company on a commercial level. It really is a matter of trying what equipment you have available and using it in short bursts as once seaweed has started to heat up it will become sticky and need drying out again in the oven before you proceed. We tried coffee grinders, spice grinders and a number of blenders and found that it depends hugely on the model of machine you have to hand. It will work fine as long as you do it slowly!

Opposite left: Some species of seaweed, such as kelp, are best dried hanging on a line.
Opposite, top right: You can use clean seawater or tap water to rinse your foraged seaweed.
Opposite, bottom right: Make sure you spread out the seaweed in a thin layer so that it can dry properly.

Top and above: You should flake or powder seaweed as soon as it is dry, before it absorbs any moisture from the atmosphere. Using a mortar and pestle gives you the greatest control over the finished texture.

Opposite: It is better to dry out rather than freeze sea spaghetti, since it goes mushy once defrosted.

Above: Be sure to thoroughly pat dry seaweed that you intend to freeze before bagging it up. The best way to freeze the thicker (brown) seaweeds is to flash-freeze them so that the cell walls do not break, and so that they do not go mushy when defrosted.

Freezing

Freezing seaweed is another way of preserving it, but it is not suitable for all types; the thinner species such as the greens, dulse and nori are good candidates. Simply treat them as you would fresh herbs: wash them, pat them as dry as possible, then freeze them from fresh in a closed freezer bag or box.

The thicker brown species such as kelp and sea spaghetti do not freeze well and behave in the same way that a cucumber would if frozen. This is because they contain so much water the crystals that form during the freezing process pierce the cells and make them mushy once defrosted.

Storing

Store dried seaweeds in a cool, dark and dry place – some species, especially the green and red types, lose their colour when exposed to direct sunlight for too long. Seaweeds also naturally contain a lot of salts, and since these are hygroscopic, they attract moisture. This trait, along with the natural tendency of seaweeds to hold moisture, means that they need to be stored in an airtight container.

If seaweed does happen to become a bit damp, simply dry it out again in the oven and it will keep again. As a general rule the lower the water content of the seaweed (or anything for that matter) the longer it will keep.

HOW TO COOK WITH SEAWEED

Each seaweed species behaves slightly differently as a result of their varying genetic make-up and cellular structure. For instance, carageen needs to be cooked in a liquid for about 15 minutes to allow the gelatinous substance to be released, whereas sea salad can be eaten raw in, as its name suggests, a salad, and the intense flavours of pepper dulse make it better suited to being employed like a herb. That said, all seaweeds are relatively straightforward to use and, as with most things, once you have had a go any inhibitions slide away! The tastes and culinary uses are wide ranging, as are the cooking methods.

When referring to 'raw' seaweeds, this could be fresh seaweed that you've foraged for and harvested, or dried seaweed that you have already rehydrated by soaking it in fresh water for 10–20 minutes.

It is important to note that not all dried seaweeds need rehydrating and it really depends on the dish you are cooking. Two things: 1) in general the thinner seaweeds do not need soaking and 2) if the dish is very 'wet' like a soup, sauce, or steams for a long time, then the seaweed will rehydrate during the cooking process.

COMMON TERMS EXPLAINED

- *Sea Salad Flakes: a mix of sea greens, dulse and nori. This is a light and very easy introduction to using seaweed as they can be sprinkled raw or cooked into any dish. They can be used as a seasoning at the end to top salads, pasta or potato dishes or sprinkled into omelettes, bread dough, casseroles and soups. They are very diverse, vibrantly coloured, and impart a subtle smoky, salty sweetness to dishes.*

- *Mixed Seaweed Flakes: usually a mix of the darker heavier seaweeds such as kelp, bladderwrack, sea spaghetti and sometimes a little dulse. This mix is a deeper, more wintery or stock-like version of sea salad, and must be cooked for the full effect. Sprinkled into soups, stews, pies or any 'wet' dish, it should rehydrate a little during cooking. It has a strong umami taste and can be used for the base of stocks or soups rather than traditional stocks.*

- *Mixed Seaweeds: a variety of seaweeds can be used where this is specified, as it does not matter which species are used. You can use a single species or a combination.*

Sea spaghetti

- Eaten raw, fresh sea spaghetti adds an asparagus-like taste and texture to dishes, and makes a wonderful crunchy addition to a salad. Be sure to rinse it well before use as the seaweed exudes a slippery, gelatinous liquid when stored for any period of time. Fresh sea spaghetti keeps well for several days in a refrigerator.

- Dried sea spaghetti is reminiscent of biltong or jerky, with the same chewy texture.

- As its name suggests, this seaweed lends itself to being served alongside or as a replacement for spaghetti. Rehydrated dried sea spaghetti is considerably softer than the fresh type, which means it cooks quickly. Bear in mind when measuring out the dried spaghetti that it swells to up to three times its dried volume when rehydrated.

- Steamed sea spaghetti will retain more texture and flavour than boiled, so this is an ideal cooking method if you are serving it alongside a main dish. Steam the rehydrated spaghetti for 20–25 minutes, until tender, or boil it for a few minutes with/instead of pasta.

- Rehydrated dried sea spaghetti also makes a delicious alternative to noodles. Simply toss it together with nearly-cooked stir-fry ingredients in a wok or pan and cook for 3–5 minutes. It will turn a rich forest-green as it heats.

Sugar kelp

- When dried this has a slightly sweet flavour but still retains a little of the saltiness, similar to kelp. It can be used in baking or bread making, as is a slightly thinner and more easily chewable version of kelp.

Bladderwrack

- A very thick tough seaweed in its whole form and not the most well known for eating, this is however a fantastic seasoning if flaked or ground finely. Fresh bladderwrack can be placed in the oven on a tray and used to bake fish, giving it a unique taste.

Opposite, top: Soaking dried sea spaghetti swells it to three times its original volume.
Opposite, bottom: Once soaked, kelp becomes supple and soft, and the process also reduces its iodine content.
Opposite right: Cooked rehydrated sea spaghetti makes a healthy and delicious alternative to spaghetti and noodles.

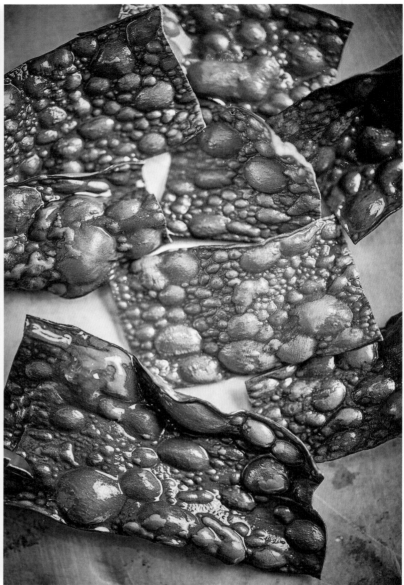

Kelp and kombu

• This is better known in Japanese or Asian cooking as kombu, and kelp in Western dishes. Kelp food supplements have been on the market for some time as a health food for bodybuilders and those interested in food supplements.

• Dried kelp has a distinctly liquorice hint to it. Some people enjoy chewing it in this form, although it is most commonly cooked in other dishes, where it imparts its umami properties before being removed at the end of the cooking time, for example when used in a stock.

Top left: A few strips of dried kelp added to the soaking water reduces both the cooking time of pulses and their unfortunate side-effects.

Above, left and above: Dried kelp and other types of seaweed can be deep-fried to produce really toothsome treats.

Opposite: Dulse can be baked or deep-fried to make tasty seaweed crisps, for recipe see page 124.

• A strip of dried kelp can be added to beans and pulses during the soaking process to speed up the subsequent cooking time and to make the pulses more digestible by breaking down the enzymes that can cause excess gas in the gut. It also imparts a subtly smoky flavour to the beans.

- Dried kelp can be deep-fat fried to make delicious crisps. Within seconds of hitting the hot oil the surface of the seaweed blisters and turns a beautiful deep green. Using a slotted spoon, immediately scoop out the crisps and set them aside on some kitchen paper to drain off excess oil.

- Kelp has a high iodine content. If consuming large quantities of kelp (over 5g dry weight at a time) the iodine content needs to be reduced first. This can be done by either soaking the seaweed in plenty of water for 20 minutes and discarding the water, or by bringing it to boiling point then discarding the water. For dishes where the kelp is simmered for a long time the iodine will evaporate naturally during the cooking process.

- Kelp can be boiled for 20 minutes until it softens, then added to any number of dishes from salads to sandwiches.

Dulse

- Dulse is famous for its strong 'umami' flavour. This leaves it with a complex, salty, nutty, smoky taste with a hint of sweetness to it and a soft, velvety texture.

- Eaten on its own, dried dulse is an excellent on-the-move snack; salty and chewy, a true taste sensation, although perhaps a bit too intense for the seaweed novice! It does not need to be rehydrated to be enjoyed like this either.

- In its raw state dulse can just be simply rinsed and then munched straight from the ocean, or chopped and used as a salad.

- Deep-fried dulse makes a fantastic crisp, and is cooked in the same way as dried kelp. It can also be coated in oil and roasted for a similar effect – try sprinkling some with smoked paprika for a smoky bacon flavour.

Pepper dulse

- Often called the 'truffle of the sea' the tiny fronds of pepper dulse range in colour from brown, through red to purple. It has an intense flavour that has been variously described as garlicky, mineral, fishy, peppery, deeply umami, and a cross between that of truffle and lobster. A little goes a long way – just as well since it is tricky to harvest!

- In its fresh form, pepper dulse can be nibbled as it is, or added sparingly all to manner of soups, stews and dishes with robust flavours, where it lends depth and enrichens the overall dish as well as seasoning it.

- Dried pepper dulse is often ground to a fine powder and used as a seasoning or spice in place of salt and pepper. The flavour intensifies as it matures so in dried form a little really does go a long way. It does not need to be soaked or rehydrated and can simply be sprinkled into sauces or dishes during cooking.

Irish moss and grape pip weed

• Irish moss or carrageen (see page 36) is largely made up of the polysaccharide carrageenan, which can be fully extracted by simmering the seaweed in a hot liquid. This results in a gelatinous substance that can be used to thicken foods, such as jellies and other desserts, as well as soups and casseroles. It is a fantastic alternative to gelatine so features widely in vegetarian or vegan cooking.

• This seaweed is a useful addition to preserves if you wish to use less sugar. The seaweed itself has very little flavour and is generally either dissolved in the dish or it can be strained to remove it before the dish is served.

• Carrageen has the property of aiding in the suspension of particles – hence its use as an emulsifier known as E407 that appears in salad dressings, milkshakes and ice cream and even toothpaste, so you may have been eating seaweed for years without knowing it!

• Carrageen is also used as a vegan alternative to finings, a settling agent in the brewing process of beers and wines traditionally made from the swim bladder of the sturgeon fish.

• The Japanese eat carrageen as a salad.

Sea lettuce and gutweed (sea greens/salad)

• Gutweed is a slightly thinner and finer species than sea lettuce.

• Dried and flaked sea lettuce and gutweeds are often packaged as sea greens or used as one of the ingredients in sea salad, which is traditionally a mix of dulse, nori and sea lettuce, greens or gutweed.

• The fresh or dried leaves are delicious raw in salads.

• Sea greens are one of the most popular seaweeds to be blended into smoothies and juices; offering a real health kick as they contain higher levels of vitamin B12 and B7 than any other plant-based food. This makes them ideal choices for vegetarians or vegans to avoid fatigue and B vitamin deficiency.

Top: With little or no taste, carrageen can be used by vegans and non-vegans to set desserts and jellies, while at the same time imparting beneficial vitamins and minerals.
Left: Dried flaked sea greens, usually a combination of sea lettuce and gutweed.
Opposite: Fresh or rehydrated wakame is delicious served simply with some sesame seeds, oil and soy sauce, or as part of a mixed salad.

Laver and nori

- This seaweed is better known as nori in Japanese or Asian cooking and as laver in Wales, where it has a strong tradition.

- The two most well-known uses of laver or nori are as the nutritious ancestral food laverbread, and as a distinctive wafer-thin wrapper for sushi. The seaweed has a high iodine, iron and protein content, and is rich in minerals and vitamins – including vitamin B12. It has a distinctive, slightly nutty flavour that some say is akin to that of oysters, and which becomes more pronounced when the seaweed is dried.

- Freshly harvested laver or nori should be washed and checked over for wildlife and shells, and then simply toasted in a dry frying pan until crisp, or spread out on a baking sheet and roasted in an oven set to 150°C/300°F/Gas 2 for 5–8 minutes. Turn the seaweed regularly and keep a close eye on it to ensure it does not burn. The crisped leaves can then be sprinkled over all manner of dishes – from soups, salsas and stir-fries to rice, pasta or grain dishes and even granola or popcorn – for a crunchy, nutritious flavour hit.

- Alternatively, marinate and tenderise the washed seaweed for about 18 hours, then add it chopped to dressings or salads.

- If you choose to make laverbread, the washed fresh seaweed must first be boiled for about 10 hours before it is mixed with other ingredients (see Seaweed Superspread on page 104). This Welsh speciality is an excellent accompaniment to cheese, butter and salty meats, though it is most commonly rolled in oatmeal to form little cakes that are fried in bacon fat. It is also frequently served with cockles, sometimes on toast – an ozone pairing made in heaven!

- Nori is most commonly available in its dried sheet form, when it ranges in colour from dark green to black, purple or dark red, and it can be bought in a range of different thicknesses. These sheets can be crumbled and used in stocks or as a seasoning, or employed for making sushi. To do the former, the sheets are first made more malleable by being slightly dampened with a cloth, and then rolled around various fillings or used in layers. Making sushi is a topic in itself, but with the ingredients and equipment now more widely available outside Japan it is well worth having a go at making some for yourself since it is a truly tasty way in which to incorporate more seaweed into your diet.

Atlantic wakame

- Known primarily in the West for its use in miso soup, wakame is predominantly produced and eaten in Japan and Korea, although it is cultivated in France and is sustainably harvested in Australia and New Zealand. With a subtle sweet and salty flavour, the soft green leaves are very high in omega-3 fatty acids, along with calcium and other nutrients, which is perhaps why it is traditional in Korea for a soup made with wakame to be consumed by women after they have given birth.

- Often sold in its dried form in the West, wakame should be rehydrated before it is included in salads, whereupon the pieces greatly increase in size. It is sometimes served on its own with sesame oil, soy sauce and a sprinkling of sesame seeds, or can be incorporated into other seaweed salads, often containing tofu.

- Wakame can also be used in soups – obviously miso, but others too – lending its briny flavour and nutrition to the dish.

SEAWEED SALT

A mixture of sea salt and dried seaweed flakes, usually dulse, nori and sea greens, this adds colour and flavour to any recipe. Not only that, as the seaweeds are high in potassium and magnesium salts (rather than just sodium) it retains a very salty flavour whilst having a lower sodium content than normal table or sea salt. Potassium and magnesium salts are much better for the body and do not have the same negative impact of regular salt.

THE RECIPES...

After digesting the wealth of seaweed information it is high time we moved on to some recipes! Within the following pages we have tried to offer a broad range of recipes to satisfy almost any palate from seafood lovers to more specialist vegan or free-from dishes. There should be something here to make most mouths water. Seaweed can take centre-stage or be used as a flavour-enhancer, you will be amazed at how versatile it is!

We have had a great bunch of friends and chefs helping to compile and shoot the final recipes with hours spent tasting and re-making most dishes to ensure the finished dish is a real treat. Kilos of melted cheese, crunchy batter, dark chocolate and fresh salads have been devoured with ease and concluded with some beautiful recipe images.

Make sure to rinse and prepare all the seaweeds as described in the previous section, unless you are using ready-prepared products.

The seaweeds specified in the recipes are chosen as we think they give best flavours in those dishes; however it is easy to substitute another seaweed if you do not have it. The seaweeds that swap easily are sea salad, pepper dulse, and sea greens. The heavier seaweeds, such as kelp, sea spaghetti or mixed seaweed flakes, can be swapped if necessary among themselves. Dulse can be interchanged with any seaweed, as it is of medium thickness and works well in most dishes.

Chapter 1
SOUPS

There's no need to wait until the colder months to enjoy these supercharged seaweed soups – they're easy both to make and to enjoy all year round, bringing nourishment and comfort on even the toughest day.

If you're new to using seaweed in cooking then there really is no better place to start. The savoury umami flavour adds a depth of flavour to any soup while at the same time providing a boost of iron, calcium, magnesium, and protein – a delicious way to re-mineralise your body.

What is more, adding seaweed to soup just makes sense since you can use whatever type you have to hand – fresh or dried – and it won't require any cooking other than that it receives in the soup pan itself.

SEAWEED FISH STOCK

Adding seaweed to a fish stock pot really boosts the taste of the finished liquid, which can then be used in all manner of fishy recipes. Use whatever dried seaweed there is to hand, and try to make the stock whenever you have some fish heads – it freezes beautifully should you not wish to use it immediately.

Makes 1 litre/1¾ pints/4 cups

1 litre/1¾ pints/4 cups water
1 carrot
1 celery stick
2–3 bay leaves
herbs and seeds of choice (eg thyme, caraway and mustard seeds)
5g/⅛oz dried seaweed or a small handful of fresh seaweed
6 fish heads

Put the water in a large pan over a medium heat and bring it to the boil.

Roughly chop the carrot (there's no need to peel it, just give it a quick wash if necessary), and the celery. Add to the pan with the remaining ingredients and simmer for about 30 minutes.

Strain the stock and use as required.

Cook's tip
Making stock is a thrifty way to use all the bits of fish and crustaceans that you'd normally discard during preparation. Simply collect them in a box and keep them in the freezer, adding to the container each time you prepare seafood, until you have enough offcuts to make up a big pan of really flavoursome stock; just increase the quantity of water, seaweed and vegetables proportionately and then portion up the strained stock and freeze it in useful quantities.

SMOKED MACKEREL & KELP DASHI STOCK

This recipe is courtesy of chef Sven-Hanson Britt, who made it when he tried some of our seaweed.
It uses the discarded mackerel skin from the Mackerel Pâté with Sea Greens recipe (see pages 116–17)
to lend fishy depth to the ozone flavour of the seaweed, and can be used as stock or the base for a noodle dish.

Makes 500ml/17fl oz/generous 2 cups

15cm/6in dried or 30cm/12in fresh kelp, or 15ml/1 tbsp mixed seaweed flakes

500ml/17fl oz/generous 2 cups water, plus extra for rehydrating dried kelp (if necessary)

3 strands dried or 5 strands fresh sea spaghetti

smoked mackerel skin

If you are using dried kelp, place it in a pan and cover it with water. Bring to the boil, then drain the seaweed in a strainer, discarding the cooking water.

Pour the measured water into the pan, then add the kelp or mixed flakes, sea spaghetti and mackerel skin. Simmer for 20 minutes.

Remove the pan from the heat and allow the stock to cool. Transfer it to a bowl, cover and place in the refrigerator to steep for at least 12 hours.

Strain the stock, removing any fat from the surface with a teaspoon or a piece of dried bread, so you are left with a clear, flavoursome stock.

TOMATO GAZPACHO WITH CRISPY SEA GREENS

A taste of summer in a bowl, this simple soup is packed with antioxidants and is smart enough for a dinner party yet speedy enough for a quick lunch. The addition of crispy sea greens as a garnish heightens not only the intense red colour of the soup, but also the punchy flavours of the ingredients, as well as providing textural interest and adding to the nutritional impact.

Put all the ingredients apart from the sea greens in a food processor or blender and blitz until smooth.

Pass the mixture through a fine strainer.

To make the crispy sea greens, heat the oil in a deep-fat fryer or small, heavy pan until the surface is shimmering. Carefully lower in the sea greens and deep-fry for about 15–30 seconds, until crispy. Be careful here as they can burn very fast. Lift out with a slotted spoon and drain on kitchen paper.

Serve the soup cold, topped with some of the crispy seaweed and a trickle of olive oil.

Serves 8

1 litre/1¾ pints/4 cups tomato juice

800g/1¾lb ripe vine tomatoes

100g/3¾oz cucumber

½ small red onion, peeled and roughly chopped

2.5ml/½ tsp fennel seeds

1 slice of white bread

30ml/2 tbsp red wine vinegar

15g/½oz basil

100ml/3½fl oz/scant ½ cup olive oil, plus extra for trickling

10ml/2 tsp salt or seaweed salt

vegetable oil, for frying

40g/1½oz fresh sea greens or 5g/⅛oz dried sea greens, rehydrated in cold water for 10 minutes

JERUSALEM ARTICHOKE & DULSE SOUP

This warming winter soup combines the creamy, nutty delights of the much underrated Jerusalem artichoke with the rich, smoky flavour of dulse, and is a perfect example of how to use dulse as a healthy alternative to cured pig-based products, such as the chorizo that is commonly paired with the tasty tuberous artichokes.

Serves 4–6

30ml/2 tbsp oil

1 large onion, peeled and diced

5ml/1 tsp ground cumin

5ml/1 tsp smoked paprika

1 celery stick, diced

1 fresh chilli, seeded if preferred and finely chopped (optional)

2 garlic cloves, peeled and finely chopped

2.5cm/1in piece of fresh root ginger, peeled and finely chopped

500g/1¼lb Jerusalem artichokes, scrubbed and chopped into 2.5cm/1in pieces

90g/3½oz fresh dulse or 15g/½oz dried dulse, roughly chopped

1 litre/1¾ pints/4 cups vegetable or seaweed stock

salt and ground black pepper, to taste

Greek (US strained plain) yogurt and chilli oil/olive oil, to garnish (optional)

Sea Greens Soda Bread (see page 263), to serve (optional)

Heat the oil in a large pan, then add the diced onion and gently caramelise over a low heat for 15–20 minutes, stirring occasionally. Cooking the onions slowly draws out the natural sugars, resulting in gorgeous golden-brown caramelisation.

Add the spices, celery and finely chopped chilli, garlic and ginger. Cook on a moderate heat for a couple of minutes to soften, then add the Jerusalem artichokes, dulse and stock.

Bring to the boil, then simmer for 30 minutes, or until the Jerusalem artichokes are soft.

Season to taste, then blend the soup until smooth.

Serve with a dollop of Greek yogurt and a trickle of oil, and some Sea Greens Soda Bread, if you like.

PORCINI & SEA SPAGHETTI BROTH

The woody, smoky flavour of the porcini mushrooms is complemented by the strong and
almost beefy taste of the sea spaghetti to create a flavoursome broth that is
great with home-made seaweed noodles.

Serves 4

1 litre/1¾ pints/4 cups water
5g/⅛oz dried porcini mushrooms
5 spring onions (scallions), sliced
20g/¾oz fresh sea spaghetti or 5g/⅛oz dried sea spaghetti, roughly chopped, or 5g/⅛oz mixed seaweed flakes
1 bay leaf
115g/4oz ramen noodles (see page 94)

Put the water in a medium pan over a medium heat
and bring to the boil.

Add the remaining ingredients and simmer for
about 30 minutes The smell of wild mushrooms
will fill the house!

Add the ramen noodles and serve immediately, or
strain the broth and use it as required in other recipes,
adding the cooked ingredients left in the strainer to a
soup or stew.

KALE, SEA GREENS & COCONUT SOUP

Delicious, healthy and very quick to make, this soup is packed with goodness from the kale and seaweed, and the addition of the dulse lends an authentic Thai fish-sauce taste while remaining vegetarian-friendly.

Serves 2

15ml/1 tbsp coconut oil

2.5cm/1in piece of fresh root ginger, peeled and finely chopped

2 garlic cloves, peeled and finely chopped

1 fresh chilli, seeded if preferred and finely chopped (optional)

1 stick of lemon grass, finely chopped

400g/14oz can of coconut milk

75g/3oz fresh sea greens or 10g/¼oz dried sea greens, roughly chopped

a large handful of kale (Russian curly kale by preference), shredded in 1cm/½in strips

25g/1oz fresh dulse or 5g/⅛oz dried dulse, roughly chopped

30ml/2 tbsp roughly chopped fresh coriander (cilantro)

juice of 1 lime

salt and ground black pepper, to taste

Heat the coconut oil in a large pan, then add the ginger, garlic, chilli and lemon grass and fry gently for a few minutes.

Add the coconut milk, swilling out the can with 200ml/7fl oz/scant 1 cup water and adding this to the pan too.

Bring to the boil, then add the sea greens, kale and dulse. Cook for 3 minutes.

Add the chopped fresh coriander and fresh lime juice. Season to taste and serve immediately.

ALL-GREEN SOUP

A real taste of spring, this is one of those great soups that essentially uses up all the odds and ends of vegetables lurking in the refrigerator, and is really healthy and full of goodness. Most green vegetables can go into it, depending upon the season, although it works very well with frozen ones, too. Sea spaghetti lends substance as well as flavour and, if you choose not to blend the soup, makes a gluten-free alternative to noodles.

Serves 4

75g/3oz fresh sea spaghetti or 10g/¼oz dried sea spaghetti

a glug of olive oil

2 leeks, sliced

2 courgettes (zucchini), diced

200g/7oz/1¾ cups frozen peas

15ml/1 tbsp mixed seaweeds

200g/7oz spinach

200g/7oz spring greens or cabbage, diced

1.3 litres/2¼ pints/5½ cups vegetable stock

a couple of handfuls of fresh basil

seaweed salt and ground black pepper, to taste

If using dried sea spaghetti, rehydrate it in cold water for 10 minutes prior to cooking. The water can be used to make up some of the stock.

Heat the olive oil in a large pan, then add the leeks and fry gently for a few minutes, until starting to soften. Add the courgettes and cook until they and the leeks are softened.

Add the peas, sea spaghetti, mixed seaweeds, spinach and spring greens or cabbage, then cover with the stock.

Bring to the boil and simmer for 20 minutes or until everything is very soft.

Add the fresh basil and blend until smooth, or leave it chunky, if you prefer. Season to taste with salt and ground black pepper and serve immediately.

BUTTERNUT SQUASH SOUP WITH SQUASH & SEA SALAD SLAW

This dish showcases the versatility of wonderfully orange sweet-tasting squash, featuring a velvet-smooth soup topped with marinated strips of raw butternut squash that have been pepped up with sea salad. A match made in squash heaven.

Serves 6–8

2 small butternut squash, peeled

a sprig of thyme

50g/2oz/¼ cup butter

1 garlic clove, peeled

1.5 litres/2½ pints/4 cups chicken stock

5g/⅛oz dried sea salad or small handful fresh mix of dulse, sea greens and/or nori, finely chopped

about 15ml/1 tbsp mayonnaise

salt and ground black pepper, to taste

olive oil, for trickling

Cut off a large chunk of butternut squash and set it aside for the slaw. Chop the remaining squash into smaller, even-size pieces so that they cook quickly and evenly.

Put the thyme, butter, garlic and chopped squash into a large pan and cook for 10–15 minutes over a low heat, until the squash is half cooked and slightly coloured.

Add the stock and bring to the boil, then simmer for about 40 minutes, until the squash is soft.

Meanwhile, make the slaw. Slice very thin strips from the large piece of reserved squash, sprinkle with salt and leave for 20 minutes (this will soften the squash). Stir in the sea salad and just enough mayonnaise to bind it together.

Blitz the soup until smooth, then add salt and ground black pepper to taste. Serve topped with some of the slaw and a trickle of olive oil.

CREAMY MUSHROOM & KELP SOUP

The umami savouriness of kelp really brings out the earthy flavour of the mushrooms in this classic soup, which is rounded out by the addition of milk and cream. Simple yet stylish, it makes a delicious autumnal treat for a cold day.

Place the kelp in a pan of water and bring to the boil. Take off the heat, strain and discard the water. Slice the kelp into strips. Reserve a few for a garnish.

Brush clean the mushrooms, then slice any larger ones so they are all about the same size, to ensure even cooking.

Heat the butter in a large pan over a medium heat, then add the mushrooms and chopped onion. Sweat down for about 10 minutes, or until the onions are softened.

Add the flour and stir to form a smooth paste. Cook for about 1 minute, then slowly add the hot stock, whisking constantly so no lumps form.

Add the sliced kelp. Simmer for 8 minutes, then turn down the heat and add the cream, milk, seasoning and nutmeg and heat for 4 minutes.

Blend the soup until smooth, then serve garnished with the reserved slices of kelp and a little olive oil trickled over the top.

Serves 4

100g/3¾oz fresh kelp or 20g/¾oz dried kelp

250g/9oz mixed mushrooms, such as shiitake, portobello, button (white)

15ml/1 tbsp butter

1 onion, peeled and finely chopped

30ml/2 tbsp plain (all-purpose) flour

450ml/¾ pint/scant 2 cups hot vegetable stock

100ml/3½fl oz/scant ½ cup double (heavy) cream

150ml/¼ pint/⅔ cup milk

salt and ground black pepper, to taste

a pinch of nutmeg

olive oil, for trickling

SMOKED MACKEREL & SPRING GREENS RAMEN

This traditional Japanese soup consists of Omega-3-rich smoked mackerel and vibrant spring greens in a wholesome seaweed stock. Served with home-made noodles, it makes a nourishing and tasty light lunch.

Serves 4

500ml/17fl oz/generous 2 cups Smoked Mackerel & Kelp Dashi Stock (see page 81)

200g/7oz spring greens, shredded

1 small leek, finely shredded

25ml/1½ tbsp rice wine vinegar

½ fresh red chilli, sliced

1cm/½in piece of fresh root ginger, finely chopped

200g/7oz smoked mackerel

a handful of seaweed, such as dulse flakes (optional)

For the ramen

115g/4oz/1 cup plain (all-purpose) flour

15ml/1 tbsp mixed seaweed flakes

1 egg

5ml/1 tsp olive oil

15ml/1 tbsp water, if necessary

First, make the ramen. Combine the flour and seaweed flakes in a bowl and make a well in the middle. Crack the egg into the well, add the olive oil and mix well. Add a small amount of water if necessary to make a soft dough.

Knead the dough on a floured surface for 5–10 minutes, or until it stops sticking to your hands so much. If you can, rest the dough in the refrigerator for several hours, or overnight if possible. This makes it easier to handle.

Flour the surfaces of the dough ball and place it between two sheets of clear film or plastic wrap, or on a floured surface. Roll out the dough as thinly as possible with a rolling pin. If you have a pasta-maker, run the dough through this several times to make it as thin as possible.

Cut the dough into fine strips and hang it on skewers or a rolling pin suspended between two items of a similar height (or over a container such as a bread bin) and leave it to dry for at least 15 minutes.

Pour the stock into a pan, bring it to a simmer and add the spring greens and leek. Simmer for 2–3 minutes.

Add the vinegar, chilli, ginger and the mackerel and simmer for 5 minutes. Add the noodles and seaweed, if using, and simmer for a further 1 minute. Serve immediately.

CULLEN SKINK WITH SEA GREENS

When Laura – who came up with this recipe – was living on a boat, she enjoyed this dish as a hearty, healthy and warming meal during the winter months. The addition of seaweed during the steeping stage enhances the creamy and smoky combination of the milk and fish, while the potatoes lend substance and turn it into a complete meal in a bowl.

Place the haddock, milk and sea greens in a pan and place over a medium heat for 10 minutes to allow the fish to absorb the flavour of the greens, and so that it will flake easily. Remove the fish with a slotted spoon and set aside.

Melt the butter in a separate pan, then add the onion and leek and sauté gently for about 10 minutes until they are soft but not coloured. Season with ground black pepper.

Add the diced potatoes and stir to coat them in the melted butter. Add the milk liquor from cooking the haddock, then simmer over a medium heat for 10–15 minutes, or until the potatoes are tender.

Meanwhile, flake the cooked haddock, checking for and removing any bones.

Mash or use a stick blender to half-blend the soup – it should have quite a chunky texture.

Add the haddock and salt and pepper to taste, and sprinkle seaweed salt over the top, if you like.

Serves 2

250g/9oz smoked haddock, preferably undyed
500ml/17fl oz/generous 2 cups milk
a handful of dried or fresh sea greens
15ml/1 tbsp butter
1 medium onion, peeled and finely diced
1 leek, thinly sliced
salt and ground black pepper, to taste
2 medium potatoes, peeled and cut into 1cm/½in cubes
seaweed salt (optional)

PHO TAI WITH KELP

With its delicious aromatic spices, this pho tai brings the smell of Asia directly into your home and tastes wonderful as a nutritious meal in a bowl. There are plenty of consommés and bone broths readily available if you don't feel like making your own, though it is worth simmering the seaweed in the bought broth to infuse the liquid with its umami goodness.

First, make the bone broth. Cut the onions and the ginger in half and brush the cut surfaces lightly with oil. Place these under a preheated grill or broiler and cook for about 15 minutes, until lightly charred. This helps to bring out the flavours.

Fill a large pan with water and bring it to the boil over a high heat. Add the bones and boil vigorously for 10 minutes, then drain, discarding the water. This helps to clean the bones and reduces the amount of scum in the finished broth. If there's marrow in the bones, use a teaspoon to scoop it out and either save it for another recipe or discard it.

Refill the pan with the cleaned bones and about 5 litres/8¾ pints/20 cups water. Bring this to the boil over a high heat, then reduce to a simmer. Using a ladle or a tea strainer, remove any scum that appears on the surface so the finished stock is as clear as possible.

Cut two squares of muslin or cheesecloth, place one on top of the other, then put all of the spices in the middle. Tie up the bundle with kitchen string and add it to the broth.

Place the kelp in a pan of water and bring to the boil, then remove from the heat and drain. Discard the water. This reduces the iodine content of the seaweed.

Add the charred ginger and onion, brisket, sugar, fish sauce, salt and kelp strip. Simmer, uncovered, for 1½ hours.

...continued overleaf

Serves 4–6

For the bone broth (makes about 4 litres/7 pints/16 cups)

2 onions

10cm/4in piece of fresh root ginger

a little oil

2kg/4½lb beef bones (knuckles work best)

1 cinnamon stick

15ml/1 tbsp coriander seeds

15ml/1 tbsp fennel seeds

5 whole star anise

1 cardamom pod

6 whole cloves

25cm/10in fresh kelp strip, or 15cm/6in dried kelp strip

500g/1¼lb piece of beef brisket

10ml/2 tsp sugar

60ml/4 tbsp fish sauce

5ml/1 tsp sea salt or seaweed salt

For the soup

250g/9oz sirloin steak

800g/1¾lb pre-cooked rice noodles

To serve

2 limes, cut into wedges

2–3 fresh chillies, seeded (if liked) and cut into wedges

2 big handfuls of fresh bean sprouts

hoisin sauce

sriracha hot sauce

a handful each of fresh mint, fresh coriander (cilantro) and fresh basil, finely shredded

Remove the meat and kelp strip and set aside. Continue to simmer the bone broth for another 1½ hours.

About 15 minutes before the end of the broth's cooking time, freeze the sirloin steak to harden it up, then slice it as thinly as you can. Cut or shred the cooked brisket meat, and set it aside. Cut the kelp into thin strips and set these aside too.

Strain the bone broth into a clean pan. Taste it and adjust the seasoning as necessary. This bit is really key, so keep trying and adjusting as required until it tastes just as you want it to.

Bring the strained broth back to a boil. Line up the soup bowls next to the pan and fill each bowl with pre-cooked rice noodles, shredded cooked brisket, the seaweed strips and the thinly sliced raw sirloin steak. As soon as the broth comes back to a boil, ladle some into each bowl. The hot broth will cook the raw beef.

Serve immediately with the limes, chilli, beansprouts, hoisin, sriracha and chopped herbs each placed in individual bowls, so guests can mix and match flavours to suit themselves.

Chapter 2
STARTERS & SNACKS

There are few better things than going out for the day knowing that you have a yummy something in your bag, especially if it'll give you an energy boost. With this in mind, we have included lots of our favourite portable picnic foods in this chapter – ones that are versatile as well as being easy to make, carry, and eat.

Other dishes are best enjoyed at home, whether for a special occasion with friends and family or just for a healthy and satisfying snack at any time. Whatever the occasion, they are sure to fit the bill, being easy to prepare yet impressive to look at, and also a little bit out of the ordinary: win win. One of the great things about adding seaweed to something you've made to share, is causing your guests to ask you what it is that makes it that extra bit delicious!

SEAWEED SUPERSPREAD

Similar to the famous Welsh laverbread, but containing other species of seaweed, this deep-green, immensely nutritious paste is a powerhouse of minerals, vitamins and protein packed into one little jar. It can be heated up and spread on hot buttered toast; mixed with oatmeal and used to make fried patties that cry out to be served with bacon and topped with an egg; added to quiches; used to stuff peppers; stirred through cooked rice with some coconut milk… It's useful stuff!

Makes 1 jar

30g/1¼oz dried sea salad or a large handful of fresh mixed sea greens, dulse and nori

20g/¾oz mixed seaweed flakes or kelp flakes

25g/1oz fresh dulse or 10g/¼oz dried dulse

15g/½oz fresh pepper dulse or 15ml/1 tbsp dried pepper dulse (optional)

1 litre/1¾ pints/4 cups water

juice of 1 lime

5ml/1 tsp white wine vinegar

ground white pepper, to taste

Put everything in a heavy pan and cook over a very low heat for about 6 hours (or cook it in a slow cooker if you have one), until it is greatly reduced and the seaweed has broken down into a paste. You may need to add more water as you go so it doesn't dry out.

Use immediately, or transfer to a sterilised jar and store in the refrigerator for up to 1 week.

DULSE & CHEESE FONDUE

Cheese is the perfect medium for showcasing the savoury depths of dulse, the addition of which both seasons and flavours this simple fondue. If the blue-cheese taste dominates too strongly, try adjusting the proportions; you can always add extra ground dulse if you want a more pronounced seaweed tang.

Serves 4–6

olive oil

1 small red onion, very finely diced

15ml/1 tbsp ground or flaked dulse

50ml/2fl oz/¼ cup white wine

400g/14oz/3½ cups grated Cheddar cheese

400g/14oz/3½oz grated Gruyère cheese

150g/5oz blue cheese, diced

ground black pepper

crusty bread and/or crudités, to serve

Coat the bottom of a frying pan with olive oil, place it over a low heat and add the diced onion and ground or flaked dulse. Cook for about 10 minutes, until the onion is softened but doesn't colour. Remove from the heat and set aside.

Place a large metal bowl over a pan of warm water over a medium heat. Add the wine and heat for 2 minutes. Stir in the cheeses, pepper and reserved onion mixture.

Keep stirring to melt the cheese and mix everything together. You may wish to add a little hot water to loosen the fondue from the edges of the bowl.

Serve immediately with crusty bread and/or crudités.

SEA SPAGHETTI-STUFFED MUSHROOMS TOPPED WITH DULSE CRUST

The simple but delicious flavour of caramelised onions is really brought out by sea spaghetti and combines perfectly with the smoky bacon-esque combination of paprika, hemp seeds and dulse, and creamy Brie. This tasty filling is then used to top meaty mushrooms, creating a satisfying and unusual light dish.

Serves 4 as a starter or 2 as a main meal

For the mushrooms

10g/¼oz dried sea spaghetti or 20g/¾oz fresh sea spaghetti

4 large flat cap mushrooms

olive oil

seaweed salt and ground black pepper, to taste

15ml/1 tbsp butter

2 medium onions, peeled and sliced

For the crust

10g/¼oz flaked dulse or 20g/¾oz fresh dulse, finely chopped

2.5ml/½ tsp smoked paprika

30ml/2 tbsp olive oil

30ml/2 tbsp hemp seeds

60ml/4 tbsp rolled oats

salt and ground black pepper (or flaked pepper dulse)

250g/9oz Brie, cut into in 1cm/½in slices

Preheat the oven to 180°C/350°F/Gas 4.

Rehydrate the sea spaghetti, if using the dried type, by soaking it in cold water for 10 minutes, then draining it. Cut the rehydrated or fresh sea spaghetti into 2.5cm-/1in-long pieces.

Wipe clean the mushrooms (don't wash them) and remove the stalks. Brush them with a little olive oil, season and roast for 15 minutes.

Warm about 15ml/1 tbsp olive oil and the butter in a heavy pan over a medium heat. Add the sliced onions and sea spaghetti, stir until fully coated, then spread out thinly over the surface of the pan.

Reduce the heat to low and cook the onions and sea spaghetti very gently for 15–20 minutes, stirring occasionally, until the onions are golden and caramelised.

Meanwhile, make the crust. In a bowl, thoroughly combine the dulse, smoked paprika, olive oil, hemp seeds, rolled oats and seasoning.

Transfer the mixture to a plate and press the crust on to one side of each of the Brie slices.

Put the mushrooms in an ovenproof dish, then top each with a little of the onion and sea spaghetti mixture, and finally top with the crusted Brie slices.

Bake for 20–30 minutes, until the mushrooms are tender and the crust is crunchy. Serve immediately.

SHRIMP CEVICHE WITH SEA SALAD POPCORN

The taste of the sea in its purest form, ceviche dishes involve 'cooking' fresh fish or seafood in acid, usually limes. Here, tender shrimp are bathed in punchy salsa flavours, and served with another South American classic – corn – which is popped with butter and seasoned with umami sea salad.

Serves 4

For the seaweed ceviche

1 red onion

salt

6 limes

30ml/2 tbsp dried sea salad or small handful of fresh dulse, sea greens or nori

500g/1¼lb shrimp or prawns, cooked and peeled

1 fresh chilli, cut in half

a bunch of fresh coriander (cilantro)

1 garlic clove, peeled

15–30ml/1–2 tbsp olive oil

For the sea salad popcorn

50g/2oz/¼ cup salted butter

15ml/1 tbsp dried sea salad

200g/7oz/1⅓ cups popcorn kernels (popping corn)

First, make the ceviche. Peel and then thinly slice the onion and place in a bowl with plenty of salt and some warm water. After 10 minutes, drain and rinse well with cold water.

Juice the limes into a bowl and add the dried sea salad, if using. Stir and leave for about 20 minutes to ensure it rehydrates. If using fresh sea salad, simply stir it in and it is ready to use immediately.

Add the shrimp, prepared onion, chilli, a few sprigs of the fresh coriander, the garlic clove, and salt to taste. Cover and leave to marinate for a couple of hours in the refrigerator.

Remove the chilli, garlic and coriander sprigs. Chop a big bunch of fresh coriander and add it to the mixture with olive oil. Taste and add additional salt if necessary.

To make the seaweed popcorn, heat the butter and sea salad in a heavy pan, ensuring the melted butter covers the base. Add the popcorn kernels and stir to coat in melted butter. Cover the pan and wait for the popping frenzy! After about 3 minutes, or whenever the popping seems to have stopped, turn off the heat.

Serve the ceviche with popcorn on the side.

DULSE & SEARED SCALLOPS

Scallops have a natural sweetness and saltiness that is perfectly balanced by the smoky umami hit of dulse. Fresh ones require minimal preparation and cooking – simply fry them quickly in hot oil until the edges are caramelised and the insides just cooked, then trickle with dulse-infused nutty browned butter. Delicious.

Serves 2

50g/2oz/¼ cup butter
15ml/1 tbsp flaked dulse or 25g/1oz fresh dulse, finely chopped
12 scallops
15ml/1 tbsp olive oil

Cook's tip
We're lucky enough to live in a place where fresh scallops are abundant, and fairly cheap, but the frozen supermarket ones are a good substitute. To use, thaw as instructed on the packet and, as for fresh ones, make sure you pat them dry with kitchen paper so that they sear rather than boil in the pan.

Put the butter in a small pan and place over a medium heat. Melt the butter, then add the dulse. Allow the butter to bubble until it browns, then reduce the heat to its lowest setting and keep warm while you cook the scallops.

Remove the hard part of scallop that attaches it to the shell, if it is still present. Some people also prefer to remove the coral, which can be used to make fish cakes, but you can leave it on if you prefer. Pat the scallops with kitchen paper so they are completely dry.

Heat the oil over a high heat in a large cast-iron or non-stick pan. Once sizzling, place each scallop in the pan and leave for 2 minutes, without moving them, before turning them over using tongs and cooking for a further 2 minutes.

Transfer the scallops to a plate, pour over the brown dulse butter and serve immediately.

DEEP-FRIED KELP-WRAPPED BRIE WITH RASPBERRY & CHILLI JAM

Used widely for wrapping sashimi in Japanese cuisine, kelp and other seaweeds can be put to great use for enclosing other foods too, such as these gooey Brie morsels. The piquant raspberry and chilli jam cuts through the richness and the contrast of flavours is a match made in heaven.

To make the raspberry and chilli jam, place the chilli and the rest of the ingredients into a pan and cook over a medium heat for 10–15 minutes, stirring frequently, until it is reduced to a jam-like consistency.

Meanwhile, rehydrate the kelp if necessary by soaking it in water for 20 minutes. Drain and pat it dry. Try to choose the thickest belts possible, since this will make wrapping easier.

Slice the Brie into six equal-size triangles.

Lay out a strip of kelp, place a Brie triangle in the middle and wrap the cheese with the seaweed, ensuring that it is completely covered. Secure the packages with cocktail sticks or toothpicks. Place some kitchen paper on a plate.

Heat the oil in a large, heavy pan over a medium heat until it is bubbling. Carefully lower the wrapped Brie triangles into the oil and deep-fry for 2–3 minutes, until the Brie is just melting inside.

Lift out the Brie triangles with a slotted spoon and drain on the kitchen paper. Serve immediately with the raspberry and chilli jam.

Cook's tip
You may need to cut the kelp strips to size so you can totally cover the brie. Using several cocktail sticks is easier. It is also good to remember that seaweed burns very fast when frying, so be careful here.

Serves 2

6 strips dried or fresh kelp

250g/9oz Brie

oil, for deep-frying

For the raspberry and chilli jam

2 fresh red chillies, seeded if preferred, finely chopped

200g/7oz fresh raspberries

30ml/2 tbsp sugar

juice of 1 lime

2.5ml/½ tsp nigella seeds

POACHED EGGS & SMOKED SALMON WITH PEPPER DULSE & SEA BEETS

A seaside take on eggs Benedict, this luxurious combination of smoked salmon, buttery wilted
sea beets seasoned with pepper dulse, and a poached egg, all bathed in velvety hollandaise sauce
or simply more melted butter, is a breakfast of champions.

If using dried pepper dulse, place it in a small cup or glass, just cover it with water and leave it to rehydrate for 20 minutes. Using a small amount of water means that the seaweed won't need to be drained, so it will retain more nutrients and flavour.

Poach the eggs. Half-fill a pan with boiling water, bring it to just below shimmering point over a medium heat and create a whirlpool using a slotted spoon. Crack one egg into a ramekin or cup and carefully slide it into the middle of the whirlpool. Wait until it has come together a bit, then repeat with the remaining eggs, taking care not to break the yolks. Cook to your preference.

Meanwhile, lay the salmon slices on to the bread.

Melt the butter in a frying pan, add the dulse and sea beets or spinach and cook briefly just to wilt down the soft leaves.

Lay the dulse and greens on top of the salmon, making a small indent in the middle in which to nestle a poached egg. Top with one egg per slice of bread and pour over some hollandaise sauce or melted butter. Sprinkle with chives, if you like, and serve immediately.

Cook's tip
If you can't get hold of pepper dulse then you can use flaked dulse, sea salad or mixed seaweed flakes which all need to be rehydrated in the same way as in the recipe.

Serves 4

15ml/1 tbsp dried or 30ml/2 tbsp fresh pepper dulse
4 eggs
200g/7oz smoked salmon
15g/½oz/1 tbsp butter
a couple of handfuls sea beets or spinach
4 slices of rye or other bread
hollandaise sauce or butter, to serve
chives, to garnish (optional)

PICKLED KELP, TOMATO & MELTED CHEESE PANINI

It takes no time to pickle kelp, and the resultant sharp, salty, umami seaweed is absolutely delicious, particularly when paired with cheese. Cheddar cheese melts well, and has a strong flavour that stands up to the pickle, but you can use any melting cheese you like.

Chop the fresh or dried kelp into small strips and soak in the vinegar in a bowl or jar for minimum of 30 minutes.

Preheat a grill or broiler to high.

Slice the tomato and some Cheddar. Arrange the panini, cut side up, on a baking sheet.

Shake off any excess vinegar from the kelp strips and arrange on top of the split panini with the tomatoes, then top with the Cheddar cheese and the herbs.

Toast under the grill until the cheese has melted, then serve immediately.

Serves 2

20g/¾oz fresh kelp or 5g/⅛oz dried kelp

50ml/2fl oz/¼ cup apple cider vinegar, or enough to cover the kelp

1 tomato

strong Cheddar cheese

2 panini rolls, split lengthways

5ml/1 tsp chopped chives or dried mixed herbs

MACKEREL PÂTÉ WITH SEA GREENS

This simple seaside pâté is greater than the sum of its carefully selected parts, and takes
no time at all to whip up, pop into a container and take on a sandy picnic. Seaweed and fish,
for obvious reasons, work extremely well together, but since smoked mackerel can be quite
salty it pays to taste the mixture as you go and start with a small quantity of dulse or seaweed salt.
Use the mackerel skins to make Smoked Mackerel & Kelp Dashi Stock (see page 81).

Serves 4

200g/7oz smoked mackerel
100g/3¾oz/8 tbsp clotted cream
10g/¼oz dried sea greens or 25g/1oz fresh sea greens
50g/2oz/4 tbsp unsalted butter
5ml/1 tsp flaked dulse or seaweed salt

Peel the skin from the mackerel and set aside (you
could make dashi with it, see page 81).

Place the fish, clotted cream and sea greens in a
blender or food processor and blitz until smooth.
Transfer the mixture to a ramekin or a lidded jar.

Melt the butter on a low heat, then add the flaked
dulse or seaweed salt and stir together. Pour the butter
to form a layer over the top of the mackerel pâté and
chill to set.

The pâté will keep for up to a week if it is well sealed
with butter. Once the seal is broken, eat within 2 days.

CHICKPEA & SEA SALAD SCOTCH EGGS

These are the most delicious gluten-free chickpea Scotch eggs, with some seaweed to give it an umami twist. Although they do take a little time and effort, this is repaid a thousandfold when you bite into the crispy coating, through the savoury outer layer to golden hidden heart. Pure picnic bliss.

Cook 4 of the eggs in a pan of boiling water for 4–6 minutes, fully immersed, to give a wonderful runny yolk. Lift out with a slotted spoon and plunge into a bowl of iced water so that they stop cooking immediately. Peel while the shell is warm.

While the the eggs are cooking, blitz the chickpeas, garlic, spring onion, tomatoes, sea salad, lime pickle and a squeeze of lemon or lime juice in a blender or food processor, until it forms a fairly fine paste. If using a stick blender, it may be a little coarse in texture, but so long as it sticks together and has a sausagemeat-like consistency then this is fine. Add a little extra lemon or lime juice as required.

Put the gram flour in a small bowl and roll each egg in it, to coat. Next, encase each of the eggs in the chickpea mixture. The easiest way to do this is to form thin patties of paste in your hands and wrap them around the eggs, patching up any holes with smaller quantities of paste.

Line up three bowls: one containing the remaining egg, beaten; one containing the remaining gram flour; and a final one containing the golden breadcrumbs.

Coat each of the eggs in turn, first in gram flour, then in egg, then in the breadcrumbs, ensuring the outside is completely coated in as even a layer of breadcrumbs as you can manage.

Put the oil into a large, heavy pan set over a medium-high heat. To test whether the oil is hot enough, drop a cube of bread into the oil; it should brown within about 30 seconds. Place some sheets of kitchen paper on a plate.

Serves 4

5 eggs
400g/14oz can chickpeas, drained
1 garlic clove, peeled
2 spring onions (scallions), roughly chopped
2 sun-dried tomatoes
15ml/1 tbsp dried sea salad
15ml/1 tbsp lime pickle, plus extra for serving
a squeeze of lemon or lime juice
115g/4oz/1 cup gram flour
100g/3¾oz/scant 2 cups golden breadcrumbs (see Cook's tip)
vegetable oil, for deep-frying

Carefully lower two eggs at a time into the oil using a slotted spoon and fry for about 4 minutes, until the outside is golden brown and crispy. Lift out and transfer to the kitchen paper while you cook the remainder of the eggs in the same way. Serve immediately, perhaps with some more lime pickle on the side.

Cook's tip
To make your own golden breadcrumbs, preheat the oven to 150°C/300°F/Gas 2. Blitz gluten-free or standard bread to your preferred consistency in a food processor; I like them quite finely ground, but you can make them slightly bigger if you prefer. Spread out the breadcrumbs on a baking sheet and toast them in the oven for about 20 minutes, shaking and stirring them halfway through and keeping a close eye on them to ensure they don't burn. Store any you don't use in an airtight container, or freeze untoasted ones in bags.

LAMB & SEA SPAGHETTI DOLMADES

This is a great make-ahead snack to serve at dinner parties and get-togethers and tastes so much better than supermarket versions. Finely chopped sea spaghetti lends another flavour dimension to the minty meat-and-rice filling and complements the distinctive taste of the vine leaves.

Finely chop the sea spaghetti, then combine all of the ingredients apart from the cabbage or vine leaves in a bowl.

Take an intact cabbage or vine leaf and place it on a surface with the veins facing upwards. Place 5–15ml/1–3 tsp of the mixture (depending on the size of the leaf) in the middle and tuck in the edges of the leaf first.

Next, roll up the leaf from the bottom to securely encase the filling. Repeat until you have used all of the filling mixture.

Place some broken cabbage or vine leaves in the bottom of a pan and arrange the dolmades on top. Cover with water, then place a weighted plate directly on top of the stuffed leaves to prevent them from floating upwards.

Simmer over a medium heat for 25 minutes, until the lamb is cooked and the rice is tender.

Leave to cool slightly and serve slightly warm, or chill until required and then bring them up to room temperature.

Variation

These dolmades can easily be made vegan by omitting the lamb and adding a handful of peas to bulk them out a little. I recommend pre-cooking this veggie filling so that it doesn't tear the leaves as you wrap it. This can be done by combining all ingredients in a pan and cooking them until the rice is soft and the water has all been absorbed.

Makes 20–25

40g/1½oz fresh sea spaghetti or 10g/¼oz dried sea spaghetti, rehydrated in cold water for 10 minutes, drained

250g/9oz minced (ground) lamb

50g/2oz/scant ¼ cup rice

1 onion, peeled and finely chopped

1 garlic clove, peeled and finely chopped

2 tomatoes, diced

a handful of fresh mint

1.25ml/¼ tsp ground cumin

100ml/3½fl oz/scant ½ cup water

25 cabbage leaves, soaked and rinsed, or vine leaves, rinsed

SEAWEED CRISPS

Crispy, intensely savoury seaweed crisps are increasingly popular, and the good news is that these ones happen to be really good for you too. To achieve the desired crunchiness it is essential that the greens are completely dry before you coat them in oil and bake them, so take some time to pat them with kitchen paper. Here are a few ideas for some variations, but once you have mastered the technique try dusting them with other seasonings, such as smoked paprika.

Dulse and kale crisps

a handful of curly kale, chopped into 4cm/1½in pieces

65g/2½oz fresh dulse or 10g/¼oz dried dulse, rehydrated in cold water for 20 minutes, chopped into 4cm/1½in pieces

15–30ml/1–2 tbsp rapeseed oil, for frying

salt and ground black pepper, to taste

Preheat the oven to 200°C/400°F/Gas 6. Toss the kale and dulse in the oil, massaging it into every nook and crevice. Add the seasoning and toss to coat evenly.

Spread out the greens in a single layer on large baking sheets lined with baking parchment and bake for about 10 minutes, stirring regularly for even cooking.

Deep-fried kelp crisps

rapeseed oil, for frying

a handful of dried kelp, chopped into 2.5–5cm/1–2in pieces

Heat enough oil to cover the seaweed in a small pan over a medium heat until the surface is bubbling. Carefully lower in a few pieces of dried kelp on a slotted spoon. They should start to sizzle within seconds.

Remove to a clean dish towel or a piece of kitchen paper to drain while you cook the remaining kelp in the same way.

Crispy sea greens

rapeseed oil, for frying

a handful of sea greens, chopped into 4cm/1½in pieces

salt

toasted sesame seeds

Heat sufficient oil to cover the sea greens in a wok or frying pan until the surface bubbles. Carefully lower in a handful of chopped sea greens and add a sprinkle of sea salt, moving regularly with a slotted spoon until crispy.

Remove to a clean dish towel or piece of kitchen paper to drain, then scatter with toasted sesame seeds.

Cook's tip
Seaweed burns very fast, especially when frying, so be very careful!

SEA SPAGHETTI BHAJIS

Seaweed bhajis were the first seaweed snack Daisy experimented with when studying at Falmouth Marine School. She originally used the invasive Japanese seaweed *Sargassum muticum* while undertaking a study on the effects on species biodiversity in areas around the Fal Estuary, but preferred the taste and texture of the sea spaghetti used here. A classic Indian dish, this is perfect as a snack, dipped in Seaweed Raita (see page 216) or served as a side dish with a curry. Bhajis are fantastic made with a range of different vegetables, such as thinly sliced broccoli and fresh garden peas, so experiment and see what floats your boat.

To make the batter, beat the gram flour, spices and seasoning with the yogurt and water in a large bowl.

Stir in the turmeric, ginger, chilli (if using) and fresh coriander and blend well, then add the sea spaghetti and onion and stir well, ensuring they are evenly coated. Line a plate with some pieces of kitchen paper.

Heat the oil in a heavy pan over a medium-high heat until it is shimmering and a small amount of batter dropped into it sizzles immediately. Working quickly and carefully, scoop up a large spoonful of the mixture and use another large spoon to slide it gently into the oil, being careful not to splash hot oil – don't slide it from too high! Repeat a few more times, so you are cooking three or four bhajis at a time, depending on the size of the pan used.

...continued overleaf

Serves 4

150g/5oz/1¼ cups gram flour
5ml/1 tsp ground cumin
5ml/1 tsp ground coriander
1.25ml/¼ tsp salt
ground black pepper
60ml/4 tbsp natural (plain) yogurt
60ml/4 tbsp water
2.5cm/1in piece of fresh turmeric, grated, or 5ml/1 tsp ground turmeric
2.5cm/1in piece of fresh root ginger, grated, or 5ml/1 tsp ground ginger
1 fresh chilli, chopped (optional)
a bunch of fresh coriander (cilantro), chopped
75g/3oz fresh sea spaghetti or 20g/¾oz dried sea spaghetti, rehydrated in cold water for 10 minutes, chopped into 5cm/2in lengths
2 small white onions, peeled and thinly sliced
vegetable oil, for frying

After about 1 minute, or when they are starting to turn golden brown, flip over the bhajis using a slotted spoon. Cook for a further minute or until golden, flipping again if necessary. Lift out with the slotted spoon and set aside on kitchen paper to drain. Repeat the process until all of the mixture is cooked. Serve immediately.

Variation

If you aren't so keen on deep-fat frying, preheat the oven to 200°C/400°F/Gas 6. Sweat off the onions in a little oil for a few minutes before adding them to the mixture, then place spoonfuls of the batter on an oiled baking sheet. Bake for about 10 minutes, trickle on a little extra oil, then bake for a further 10 minutes, until golden and crunchy.

COURGETTE & DULSE FRITTERS

With its bacon-like flavour, the inclusion of dulse in these fritters means they could be enjoyed for breakfast topped with a poached or fried egg. They partner especially well with a chutney or spicy dipping sauce for a tasty snack or appetiser at other times of the day.

Makes about 16

1 large courgette (zucchini)
1 small or ½ large red onion
75g/3oz fresh dulse or 20g/¾oz dried dulse, rehydrated in a small amount of cold water for 20 minutes, chopped into 5cm/2in lengths
150g/5oz/scant 1 cup drained canned corn
350g/12oz/3 cups gram flour
10ml/2 tsp ground cumin
5ml/1 tsp ground turmeric
15ml/1 tbsp lemon juice
2.5ml/½ tsp salt
2.5ml/½ tsp baking powder
120ml/4fl oz/½ cup water
30ml/2 tbsp coconut oil, for frying
poached eggs, to serve (optional)

Grate the courgette and peel and finely dice the onion, then put them in a big mixing bowl. Alternatively, use a mini food processor to finely chop them both.

Add the dulse, corn and 275g/10oz/2½ cups of the gram flour along with the cumin, turmeric, lemon juice, salt and baking powder. Mix well to combine.

Slowly add the water a little at a time and mix until you achieve a lumpy dough that is thick enough to be rolled out. Adjust the consistency by adding more of the remaining chickpea flour if it feels too sloppy.

Cover the bowl with a clean dish towel and leave the dough to rest for at least 30 minutes.

Place the dough between two sheets of baking parchment and roll it out until it is 5mm/¼in thick. Stamp out rounds using a cookie cutter or the rim of a glass.

Put half of the coconut oil in a large frying pan and place it over a medium heat. When the oil is hot, carefully slide in about four fritters using a spatula.

Let the fritters cook for 4–5 minutes or until golden on one side before turning them very carefully and cooking them until they are golden on the other side, too. It's important not to let the fritters overcook or they will be dry.

Transfer the cooked fritters to a plate and continue cooking in batches until all of the mixture has been used. Serve hot, with a poached egg on top, if you like.

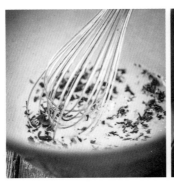

SEA SALAD-BATTERED ROCK SALMON GOUJONS

These tasty sea-salad-seasoned goujons are a great way to use sustainable, locally caught fish, the simple treatment making the fish the star of the show. Dogfish, or rock salmon, suggested here, has little commercial value largely due to the difficulty of peeling off its skin, but if you are able to get hold of it ready-prepared it has a delicious meaty texture. Alternatively, use any sustainable meaty white fish that has been sourced locally.

Serves 2

about 300g/11oz rock salmon fillets or fillets from other sustainable fish, skinned

rapeseed oil, for frying

Dulse and Kale Crisps (see page 124), Caper, Pepper Dulse & Horseradish Dressing (see page 218) and toasted sourdough, to serve (optional)

For the batter

60ml/4 tbsp flour, plus extra for coating the fish

30ml/2 tbsp sea salad flakes

150ml/¼ pint/⅔ cup water or milk

salt and ground black pepper, to taste

Cook's tip

An alternative to fishing out (no pun intended!) the cooked goujons from the hot oil is to drain them through a heatproof strainer positioned over a heatproof bowl or a large pan to catch the oil. Whichever means you use, take great care when cooking with hot oil.

Whisk together all of the batter ingredients in a large bowl and set aside.

Cut the fish into 1cm-/½in-wide strips and roll in flour to coat all over. Set aside.

Heat the oil in a heavy pan over a medium heat. To test whether it is up to temperature, drip in a little batter; it should start bubbling and turning golden immediately. Place some sheets of kitchen paper on a plate.

Dip the floured fish into the batter and carefully lay the strips into the hot oil or use a slotted spoon to lower them in. Take great care and do not overcrowd the pan; cook the fish in several batches if necessary.

Leave to cook for 1–2 minutes, until the batter is golden brown, then transfer to the kitchen paper to drain.

Serve hot, with whichever accompaniments you prefer. Try the Caper, Pepper Dulse and Horseradish Sauce on page 218!

Chapter 3
MAIN COURSES

Here we've put together our favourite tried (and happily) tested main-course recipes. Drawn from numerous cuisines from around the world, you'll find plenty of ideas for wholesome yet elegant dishes that make the most of land and sea.

There is an abundance of amazingly delicious and healthy produce to be found on our shores but it is all too often overlooked; this chapter shows that seaweed really can be a kitchen staple.

Once we had fully embraced seaweed as a key ingredient, we were so enthused that it was easy to come up with imaginative ways to incorporate it into our daily diet. We hope that the fruits of our labours will inspire you to try out something new, and also give you the confidence to experiment yourself.

VEGETABLE SEAWEED DAAL

Packed with protein and nutrients, daal is a staple food in many parts of the world,
either served as an accompaniment or a main course. Here, the Asian flavours are given a boost by
the addition of kelp, while the vegetables lend colour and interest and turn this into
a hearty and healthy meal in a bowl.

Serves 2 as a main course, or 4 as an accompaniment

50g/2oz fresh kelp or 20g/¾oz dried kelp, rehydrated in cold water for
30 minutes, then drained, or 15ml/1 tbsp mixed seaweed flakes

15ml/1 tbsp olive oil

1 onion, peeled and sliced, plus a few extra slices to garnish

2 garlic cloves, peeled and chopped

a 2.5cm/1in piece of fresh root ginger, peeled and chopped

5 fresh curry leaves

10ml/2 tsp ground ginger

5ml/1 tsp ground turmeric

5ml/1 tsp ground cumin

5ml/1 tsp garam masala

400ml/14fl oz/1⅔ cups vegetable stock

400g/14oz canned tomatoes

1 medium potato, peeled and diced

1 carrot, peeled and diced

½ cauliflower, broken into small florets

a handful of frozen peas

150g/5oz/scant ¾ cup brown, green or orange dried lentils,
soaked as required

a handful of fresh coriander (cilantro), shredded, to garnish

rice or another curry, to serve

Slice the kelp into 1cm/½in pieces.

Heat the oil in a large pan or wok, then add the onion and cook over a medium heat for 5 minutes. Add the garlic and fresh root ginger and cook for a further 5 minutes, until the onion is soft.

Add the curry leaves and fry for 30 seconds, then add the ground spices and fry for 1 minute over a low heat.

Pour in the stock, tomatoes, potato, carrot, cauliflower, peas, kelp and lentils and simmer for 20 minutes or until the vegetables and lentils are soft, stirring regularly. Add a drop more water if necessary.

Garnish with fresh coriander and onion slices, and serve with rice or another curry dish if it is an accompaniment.

KELP VEGETABLE CHILLI

Few things are as comforting as a steaming bowl of fragrant chilli on a cold winter's night, and this vegetarian one is as nutritious as it is tasty. Packed with storecupboard staples and everyday veg, it is also likely to be something you can throw together with what you have in the house and, unlike its meaty counterpart, it doesn't require hours of cooking since the smoked-bacon taste of the kelp lends sufficient depth of flavour in just half an hour.

Heat the oil over a medium heat in a heavy casserole or deep pan, then add the onion, garlic and carrot and fry for 6–8 minutes, until starting to soften.

Add the peppers and fry for a further 1 minute, then add the mushrooms and fry for 4 minutes, until all of the vegetables are softened.

Add the spices and fry for 1 minute, until fragrant, then add all the remaining ingredients, reserving a few strips of kelp for a garnish. Stir to combine well.

Simmer for 25 minutes or until the vegetables are soft and the liquid has mostly cooked off.

Serve with a dollop of Greek yogurt, if you like.

Serves 4

5ml/1 tsp olive oil

1 onion, peeled and chopped

2 garlic cloves, peeled and chopped

2 carrots, peeled and chopped

½ green (bell) pepper, seeded and chopped

1 red (bell) pepper, seeded and chopped

100g/3¾oz mushrooms, wiped clean and diced

5ml/1 tsp curry powder (or adjusted to taste)

400g/14oz can chopped tomatoes

400g/14oz can red kidney beans in water, drained

400g/14oz can corn, drained

10ml/2 tsp ground cumin

10ml/2 tsp dried oregano

5ml/1 tsp ground cinnamon

5ml/1 tsp paprika

2.5ml/½ tsp chilli powder (or more if desired)

a pinch of salt and ground black pepper

60g/2¼oz fresh kelp or 25g/1oz dried kelp, soaked in cold water for 30 minutes then drained, cut into thin strips

a dollop of Greek (US strained plain) yogurt, to serve (optional)

BEETROOT, MUSHROOM & DULSE BURGERS

Gone are the days when veggie burgers need to be dull affairs; these lively, nutrient-packed beauties seasoned with the sea are so delicious they will sway even the most dedicated meat-eater, and they are very easy to throw together and cook. NB, they are not as robust as meat burgers, so if you want to cook them on a barbecue then it would be best to put a suitable frying pan on the barbecue rack and cook them in that, rather than placing them directly on the bars.

Makes 8–10 burgers

4 raw beetroots (beets), grated

1 small red onion, peeled and finely chopped

2 garlic cloves, peeled and finely chopped

200g/7oz button (white) mushrooms (or whatever you have to hand), wiped clean and finely chopped

10g/¼oz flaked dulse or 65g/2½oz fresh dulse, finely chopped

130g/4½oz/1½ cups rolled oats

15ml/1 tbsp olive oil

2 eggs or 30ml/2 tbsp chia seeds soaked for 15 minutes in 150ml/ ¼ pint/⅔ cup water

a handful of fresh basil or 5ml/1 tsp dried basil

a pinch of seaweed salt and ground black pepper or pepper dulse

50g/2oz/½ cup plain (all-purpose) flour (use spelt flour if you prefer)

coconut or other oil of choice, for frying

8–10 burger buns

For the toppings

a squeeze of lemon, slices of avocado, slices of tomato and shredded iceberg lettuce OR a squeeze of lemon, red onion rings, watercress or baby spinach, and English mustard

Place the beetroot, onion, garlic and mushrooms in a large bowl, then add the flaked dulse or chopped fresh dulse, oats, oil, eggs or chia, basil, salt, pepper or pepper dulse, and flour.

Mix together well and leave to sit for at least half an hour so the oats can soften and soak up the flavours.

After 30 minutes, try forming a burger with your hands. If it gives off too much water, add a little flour until you achieve a consistency that is not too watery but is not so dry it falls apart.

Cook's tip
The burger mixture can be frozen (before it is formed into burgers) but note that when it is defrosted it tends to be more watery, so you will probably need to add some more flour before forming it into burgers.

...continued overleaf

Heat the oil in a large frying pan on a medium high heat. Once the oil is hot, form a burger in your hands and place it gently into the frying pan, pressing it down so it is about 1cm/½in thick. Repeat with the remaining mixture. You will probably need to form and then cook the mixture in several batches since it is best not to overcrowd the pan.

Fry the burger for 4-5 minutes on one side or until it starts to turn golden, then carefully flip it over and let it cook for a further 4 minutes or so on the other side. Turn over the burger two more times and cook it for a couple of minutes more on each side to make sure it is cooked all the way through. Take care not to let it burn.

Remove the cooked burgers to a plate and keep warm while you cook the remaining burgers in the same way.

Serve each in a burger bun with a squeeze of lemon on top followed by the toppings of your choice.

SEA ALOO

This pretty bowl is brimful of goodness and is as pleasing to eat as it is on the eye. Seaweed works brilliantly with most spiced dishes, the earthy umami bringing out the nuances of the other flavours, and in this dish it also perfectly complements the spinach and tender new potatoes.

Serves 4

5ml/1 tsp cumin seeds
5ml/1 tsp mustard seeds
15–30ml/1–2 tbsp vegetable oil
1 large white onion, peeled and sliced
1cm/½in piece of fresh root ginger, finely grated
1cm/½in piece of fresh turmeric, finely grated, or 1.25ml/½ tsp ground turmeric
1 fresh chilli (optional)
2 garlic cloves, peeled and crushed
3 tomatoes, diced
500g/1¼lb new potatoes, scrubbed if necessary and halved
seaweed salt and ground black pepper, to taste
15g/½oz dried sea salad, sea greens or dulse, or large handful fresh seaweed, roughly chopped
65g/2½oz fresh dulse, roughly chopped or 10g/¼oz flaked dulse
5ml/1 tsp garam masala
200g/7oz baby leaf spinach

Heat a dry, heavy pan over a low heat, add the cumin and mustard seeds and toast for a couple of minutes, until they start popping and smell aromatic.

Remove from the heat and lightly crush the toasted seeds in a pestle and mortar or give them a quick whizz in a spice grinder, until they are coarsely ground.

Pour the oil into the pan and place over a medium heat, then add the onion, toasted spices, ginger, turmeric and chilli (if using). Cook for a few minutes, until the onions are starting to soften.

Add the garlic and tomatoes and cook for a further few minutes, until both are starting to soften. Now add the potatoes, season well and add a splash of water.

Put on the lid, turn down the heat and allow the mixture to simmer, stirring regularly and adding water as necessary so that the potatoes don't dry out.

When the potatoes are nearly cooked, add the seaweeds. Replace the lid and cook for a couple of minutes so the greens can rehydrate in the steam – make sure there is still moisture in the pan but bear in mind this is traditionally a dry-ish dish.

Finally, stir in the garam masala and baby leaf spinach, replace the lid and cook briefly, until the spinach has just wilted over the potatoes. Serve immediately.

SEA SALAD MOUSSAKA

This is a seaweed spin on a classic moussaka in which the slightly charred aubergine lends a smoky depth of flavour that is complemented by the generous inclusion of flaked sea salad. It's a good one to make ahead when you have time, ready to popped into a hot oven after a busy day.

Serves 4

90ml/6 tbsp olive oil, plus extra for greasing

1–2 large aubergines (eggplants), about 500g/1¼lb, chopped into 2.5cm/1in pieces

seaweed salt and ground black pepper, to taste

60ml/4 tbsp flaked sea salad

2 onions, peeled and chopped

2 garlic cloves, peeled and chopped

450g/1lb minced (ground) lamb or beef

400g/14oz can chopped tomatoes

10ml/2 tsp tomato paste

15ml/1 tbsp mixed seaweed flakes

10ml/2 tsp fresh oregano (or 5ml/1 tsp dried oregano)

15g/½oz fresh flat leaf parsley, chopped

5ml/1 tsp ground cinnamon

125g/4½oz feta cheese

250g/9oz ricotta

1 egg

Preheat the oven to its highest temperature (about 240°C/475°F/Gas 9). Grease a medium-size ovenproof dish with a little olive oil.

Put the aubergine pieces in a bowl with 60ml/4 tbsp of the olive oil, salt and pepper, and 30ml/2 tbsp of the flaked sea salad. Stir to thoroughly coat the aubergine pieces with oil, then spread them out on a baking sheet and roast in the hot oven for 25 minutes, until soft and slightly charred.

Transfer the aubergines to the greased oven dish and spread them out evenly. Reduce the oven temperature to 200°C/400°F/Gas 6.

Heat the remaining oil in a large pan over a medium heat, add the onion and cook for 5 minutes. Stir in the garlic and meat and cook for about 6 minutes or until the meat is browned, stirring all the time to prevent the mixture from catching.

Add the tomatoes, tomato paste, remaining flaked sea salad, mixed seaweed flakes, oregano, chopped parsley, cinnamon, and a generous pinch of salt and pepper.

Stir to combine, then simmer, stirring the mixture regularly, for 15 minutes. Pour the mixture evenly over the aubergine pieces in the oven dish.

Crumble the feta into a bowl and mix in the ricotta, egg and a pinch of salt and pepper, then spread the sauce evenly over the top of the tomato mixture.

Put the dish in the oven and bake for about 15 minutes, until the topping is bubbling and browned.

SEAWEED LAX PUDDEN

This is our take on a Swedish comfort-food dish that is a little like a smoked salmon tortilla.
Adding some sea greens really brings out the taste of the fish, but since it also brings salinity,
unsmoked salmon is used in this recipe and there is no need for additional salt.

Preheat the oven to 160°C/325°F/Gas 3. Grease a high-sided ovenproof dish with a little melted butter.

Peel and thinly slice the potatoes, then place them in a medium pan and cover with cold water. Bring to the boil and cook for 8 minutes, until they are just tender.

Drain the potatoes, then rinse them under cold water. Drain again and spread them out on a clean dish towel, patting them dry with another clean dish towel.

Put the eggs, milk, cream, 2.5ml/½ tsp each of salt and pepper, the sea greens and the 30g/1oz/ 2 tbsp melted butter into a large bowl. Whisk to combine thoroughly.

Layer around one-third of the potatoes on the base of the buttered dish, then spread half of the salmon and dill over the top. Add another layer of potatoes, the rest of the salmon and most of the remaining dill, and finally top with the remaining one-third of the sliced potatoes.

Pour over the whisked egg custard, sprinkle with the remaining dill and grind over some black pepper.

Bake for 45 minutes until the custard is set, then serve with a salad and some bread.

Serves 4

30g/1oz/2 tbsp unsalted butter, melted, plus extra to grease

675g/1½lb waxy potatoes

4 eggs

300ml/½ pint/1¼ cups whole milk

100ml/3½fl oz/scant ½ cup double (heavy) cream

salt and ground black pepper, to taste

15g/½oz dried sea greens or 65g/2½oz fresh sea greens, chopped

250g/9oz salmon fillet, deboned and cut into small chunks

20g/¾oz fresh dill, chopped

salad and bread, to serve

SEA SALAD & BROCCOLI QUICHE

Seasoned with flecks of sea salad and packed with vivid-green broccoli, this appetising quiche doesn't contain any cream, so is healthier than many other recipes. It is equally lovely served warm for dinner or cold for lunches or picnics with a little crunchy salad on the side. For a super-speedy version, use 375g/13oz good-quality ready-made shortcrust pastry.

First make the pastry. Put the flour and salt into a large bowl, then add the cubed cold butter and rub with your fingers until the mixture resembles fine breadcrumbs.

With a blunt knife, mix in the water a few drops at a time until the mixture starts to form clumps, then knead it gently for a few seconds and roll it into a ball. Alternatively, you could make the pastry by placing all the ingredients in a food processor – just make sure you don't overwork it and stop as soon as it comes together into a ball.

Wrap the pastry ball in clear film or plastic wrap and chill in the refrigerator for 30 minutes.

Put a baking sheet in the oven and preheat it to 200°C/ 400°F/Gas 6. Grease a 25cm/10in flan dish or pan.

Roll out the pastry on a lightly floured surface to a thickness of about 3mm/⅛in and large enough so that it will fill the base and sides of the flan dish or pan.

...continued overleaf

Serves 6–8

For the shortcrust pastry

250g/9oz/2¼ cups plain (all-purpose) flour

a pinch of salt

125g/4½oz/generous ½ cup cold unsalted butter, cubed

about 45ml/3 tbsp cold water

For the filling

15ml/1 tbsp olive oil, plus extra for greasing

1 onion, peeled and finely chopped

2 garlic cloves, peeled and finely chopped

3 large (US extra large) eggs

120ml/4fl oz/½ cup milk

5ml/1 tsp chives

a pinch of salt and ground black pepper

1 large head of broccoli, cut into small florets

90g/3½oz/¾ cup grated Cheddar cheese

handful of roughly chopped fresh seaweed, such as sea lettuce, nori and/or dulse, or 10ml/2 tsp flaked sea salad

Drape the pastry over the rolling pin and gently place it in the dish or pan, pressing down around the edge of the base so it fits neatly. Do not trim away the edges of the pastry where they overhang – doing it once the pastry has been blind-baked ensures the best finish.

Scrunch up a large piece of baking parchment or foil and fit it over the pastry, then fill with baking beans or uncooked rice to weight down the pastry.

Put the pastry case on the hot baking sheet (this will ensure the base of the pastry cooks properly and also catches any spills once you have filled the quiche) and blind-bake it for about 15 minutes. Remove the baking parchment or foil and the beans or rice and return the uncovered pastry case to the oven to bake for a further 5 minutes.

Meanwhile, prepare the filling. Heat the oil in a frying pan over a medium heat, add the onion and sauté for about 10 minutes, until soft. Add the garlic and cook for 2–3 minutes.

Beat together the eggs and milk in a bowl, then add the chives, salt and pepper.

Remove the pastry case from the oven, still on the baking sheet, at the end of its cooking time.

Spoon the onion, garlic and broccoli into the base, then sprinkle over half of the cheese. Pour over the egg mixture, then sprinkle with the flaked sea salad or roughly chopped fresh seaweed, and the remaining cheese.

Carefully slide the baking sheet and quiche back into the oven and reduce the temperature to 180°C/ 350°F/Gas 4. Bake for about 25 minutes or until the filling has set and the cheese has turned a lovely golden colour.

Remove from the oven and trim away the overhanging pastry. Leave to cool at least slightly, or until cold, then remove the quiche from the dish or pan and cut it into wedges for serving.

DAIRY-FREE SEAWEED & VEGETABLE QUICHE

Quiches are often rather rich affairs, packed with saturated fat and laden with dairy products; not something those who need to avoid dairy can usually enjoy! This version, however, is made with a double dose of health-boosting seaweed in the form of sea spaghetti and sea salad.

Put a baking sheet in the oven and preheat it to 200°C/400°F/Gas 6. Grease a 20cm/8in flan dish or pan with a little oil.

Make the pastry as described on page 151, and chill. Roll out the pastry on a lightly floured surface to a thickness of about 3mm/⅛in and large enough so that it will fill the base and sides of the flan dish or pan.

Drape the pastry over the rolling pin and gently place it in the dish or pan, pressing down around the edge of the base so it fits neatly. Do not trim away the edges of the pastry where they overhang – doing it once the pastry has been blind-baked ensures the best finish.

Scrunch up a large piece of baking parchment or foil and fit it over the pastry, then fill with baking beans or uncooked rice to weight down the pastry.

Put the pastry case on the hot baking sheet (this will ensure the base of the pastry cooks properly and also catches any spills once you have filled the quiche) and blind-bake it for about 15 minutes. Remove the baking parchment or foil and the beans or rice and return to the oven to bake for a further 5 minutes.

Meanwhile, prepare the filling. If using dried sea spaghetti, place it in a small bowl, add enough water to just cover and leave it to rehydrate for 10 minutes. Drain. Chop whichever type of sea spaghetti you are using into 2.5cm/1in lengths.

Heat the oil in a frying pan over a medium heat, add the onion and sauté for 10 minutes, until soft.

Add the pepper, courgette, mushrooms and sea spaghetti and cook until just softened, stirring occasionally, then add the garlic, sea salad and tomatoes and cook for 1 minute.

Beat together the eggs, milk and salt and pepper in a bowl. Remove the cooked pastry case from the oven, still on the baking sheet, at the end of its cooking time.

Serves 4–6

15ml/1 tbsp olive oil, plus extra for greasing
300g/11oz dairy-free pastry (see recipe on p151, substituting dairy-free spread for butter)
5g/⅛oz dried sea spaghetti or 20g/¾oz fresh sea spaghetti
1 onion, peeled and finely chopped
1 red (bell) pepper, seeded and finely chopped
1 small courgette (zucchini), finely chopped
75g/3oz mushrooms, wiped clean and sliced
2 garlic cloves, peeled and finely chopped
5g/⅛oz flaked sea salad
7 cherry tomatoes, halved
3 large (US extra large) eggs
150ml/¼ pint/⅔ cup unsweetened soya milk
a pinch of seaweed salt and ground black pepper
50g/2oz/½ cup grated dairy-free cheese
a few sprigs of fresh dulse, sea greens or nori
6 asparagus spears, pitted black olives and/or roughly chopped sun-dried tomatoes (optional)

Spoon the softened vegetables into the base of the pastry case and spread them out evenly, then sprinkle with the cheese and the sprigs of seaweed.

Pour over the egg mixture, then arrange the asparagus, olives or sun-dried tomatoes on top, if you wish to use them – this isn't essential, but they all add extra flavour if you happen to have them to hand.

Carefully slide the baking sheet and quiche back into the oven and reduce the temperature to 180°C/350°F/Gas 4. Bake the quiche for about 25 minutes or until the filling has just set and the top is golden.

Remove the quiche from the oven and trim away the excess pastry. Leave it to cool at least slightly, or until it is completely cold. It is best not to eat it when it is piping hot. Remove the quiche from the dish or pan and cut it into wedges for serving.

LEEK, MUSHROOM & DULSE OMELETTE

The beauty of omelettes is that they are quick and simple to prepare and can be enjoyed hot or cold. They are also almost infinite in their variety, so feel free to experiment with different types of seaweed as well as other cheeses, seeds and vegetables. This dish feeds two when served with a crisp fresh salad and new potatoes.

Serves 2

15ml/1 tbsp butter

½ onion, peeled and diced

4 button (white) mushrooms, sliced

1 small leek, sliced into 1cm-/½in-wide rings

1 garlic clove, peeled and crushed (optional)

4 eggs

a splash of milk (or 30ml/2 tbsp crème fraîche for an extra-rich omelette)

65g/2½oz fresh dulse or 10g/¼oz dried dulse, rehydrated in a little water for 5 minutes, chopped into 2.5cm/1in-long pieces

seaweed salt and ground black pepper, to taste

5cm/2in piece of a goat's cheese log, cut into pieces

15ml/1 tbsp sunflower and/or pumpkin seeds

Preheat the grill or broiler to medium. Melt the butter in a 25cm/5in frying pan over a medium heat. Add the onion and sauté for 5 minutes, then add the mushrooms and cook until golden.

Stir in the leek and garlic (if using) and cook for a further couple of minutes, until the leek is softened.

Lightly beat the eggs in a bowl, then stir in the milk and dulse, season well and add to the pan.

Cook on a low heat for about 3 minutes, until bubbles start appearing on the surface. Arrange the cheese on top, sprinkle with seeds and place under the grill, until the cheese is melted and the omelette is set and golden.

SEA PANEER OR TOFU

The idea for this recipe came from the Indian dish saag paneer (fried spinach and fresh cheese), but this one offers an option to make it suitable for vegans by using tofu in place of the paneer, and switching the single cream with coconut milk. Finally, you can add some seaweed in with the spinach. If you are able to forage for your own dulse, you can substitute more of the spinach with the seaweed – just make sure you taste it before you add any additional salt.

Heat a glug of olive oil in a frying pan over a medium-high heat, add the paneer or tofu and fry, turning carefully and frequently using kitchen tongs, for about 5 minutes or until the cubes are golden all over. Transfer to a piece of kitchen paper to drain. Set aside.

Reheat the pan in which the paneer or tofu was fried and add the cumin seeds. Cook for 1 minute.

Add the diced onion and cook gently for about 10 minutes, until softened, then stir in the garlic, ginger, garam masala and turmeric.

Cut the tomato in half and seed it, then finely chop it. Add this to the pan and cook for a further 10 minutes. If you use a tinned tomato, reduce the time to 5 minutes.

Add the spinach, cover and cook for a few minutes, then stir in the cream or coconut milk, paneer or tofu, and the fresh or dried dulse.

Reduce the heat and simmer for 5 minutes with the lid off, so the cream starts to thicken. Season to taste and serve.

Serves 4

olive oil

200g/7oz paneer or tofu, cut into roughly 2cm/¾in cubes or pieces

5ml/1 tsp cumin seeds

1 onion, peeled and finely chopped

2 garlic cloves, peeled and finely chopped

1cm/½in piece of fresh ginger root, peeled and chopped

10ml/2 tsp garam masala

2.5ml/½ tsp turmeric

1 ripe tomato/canned tomato

300g/11oz frozen or fresh spinach

50ml/2fl oz/¼ cup single (light) cream or coconut milk

30g/1½oz dried dulse or 185g/6½oz fresh dulse, cut into strips

seaweed salt and ground black pepper, to taste

MARINATED FISH & KELP CURRY

Marinating fish and kelp with curry paste and acidic lemon juice helps to tenderise them and reduces the cooking time, meaning fewer nutrients are destroyed by the heat. It also gives the curry greater depth of flavour, really bringing the marine tang to the fore.

Soak the kelp in a bowl of cold water for 20 minutes. Drain. Slice the kelp into small strips.

Put half of the curry paste in a non-reactive dish, then squeeze over the juice from half of the lemon and stir to combine.

Add the fish and most of the the kelp and massage with the paste to ensure it completely coats them. Cover and leave to marinate in the refrigerator for at least 30 minutes.

Heat the oil in a deep pan over a medium heat, then add the onion, garlic and ginger and gently fry for about 10 minutes, until the onion is soft.

Add the remaining curry paste and the chilli and stir-fry for 1–2 minutes, then pour in the tomatoes and stock.

Bring to a simmer, then add the fish and kelp along with the marinade. Gently cook for 4–5 minutes, or until the fish is cooked through and flakes easily.

Garnish the cooked rice with the reserved kelp strips, then serve with the curry and yogurt.

Serves 4

10g/¼oz dried kelp or 40g/1½oz fresh kelp
30ml/2 tbsp Madras curry paste
1 lemon, halved
500g/1¼lb sustainable white fish fillets, skinned and cut into big chunks
15ml/1 tbsp olive oil
1 large onion, peeled and finely chopped
1 garlic clove, peeled and finely chopped
a 5cm/2in piece of fresh root ginger, peeled and finely chopped
1 fresh red chilli, seeded if preferred, finely chopped
400g/14oz canned tomatoes
200ml/7fl oz/scant 1 cup vegetable stock
cooked rice and natural (plain) yogurt, to serve

THAI FISH & SEAWEED PIE

Marrying salty, sweet and spicy flavourings, this Thai-inspired fish pie makes a welcome change from its creamy traditional counterpart and is packed with beneficial ingredients. It is also extremely easy and quick to put together, and can be assembled in advance and then baked when required, the slow-cooking drawing out the natural sweetness of the butternut squash and carrot and allowing time for the umami seaweed flavour to infuse the coconut-milk sauce.

Serves 6

4 large potatoes, peeled and diced

30ml/2 tbsp butter, plus extra for brushing the pie

salt and ground black pepper, to taste

3 large carrots, peeled and grated

500g/1¼lb smoked haddock and 500g/1¼lb white fish, skinned, deboned and chopped into chunks

75g/3oz fresh sea spaghetti or 20g/¾oz dried sea spaghetti, chopped into 2.5cm/1in lengths

40g/1½oz fresh dulse or 10g/¼oz dried dulse, roughly chopped

½ butternut squash, peeled and chopped into large chunks

12 cherry tomatoes, halved

a large handful of spinach

400ml/14oz can coconut milk

a small bunch of fresh coriander (cilantro), finely chopped

1cm/½in piece of fresh root ginger, peeled and finely grated

1 stick of lemongrass, finely chopped

1 garlic clove, peeled and finely chopped

1 small fresh red chilli, seeded and finely chopped (optional)

lime wedges, to serve

Boil or steam the potatoes until soft, then drain and mash with the butter and seasoning. Stir in the grated carrot.

Preheat the oven to 180°C/350°F/Gas 4. Combine the remaining ingredients, apart from the lime wedges, in a large ovenproof dish and season lightly.

Spoon the mashed potato and carrot mixture evenly over the surface, then brush the surface with butter.

Bake for about 1¼ hours, until the top has turned a lovely golden brown. Serve in shallow bowls with lime wedges for squeezing over.

Variation

Replace the fresh coriander (cilantro) with fresh dill and parsley, and replace the ginger, lemongrass, garlic and chilli with 115g/4oz/1 cup grated strong Cheddar cheese and 300ml/½ pint/1¼ cups milk. Top with more grated cheese.

FISH SEAWEED PAELLA

Having lived in the Valencia region of Spain, Laura was always pleased to see on the daily menu board the words arròz a banda – essentially a type of paella that uses surf and turf. In reality, the great thing about paella is that the ingredients can vary to suit what's available. Here, the seaweed brings a depth of flavour and is used primarily as a seasoning, although it adds glistening colour too.

First, fillet the fish, reserving the offcuts for the stock. To make the stock, place the fish heads and bones, 8 of the mussels (discarding any open mussels that don't close when sharply tapped), ½ onion, mixed seaweed flakes, the bay leaf, 1 garlic clove, the paprika and 1 roughly chopped tomato into a large pan. Add the water and wine and bring to the boil. Reduce the heat and simmer, uncovered, for 45 minutes.

Grind the remaining 3 garlic cloves in a mortar with a pinch of salt and 7.5ml/½ tbsp of the olive oil. If you don't have a mortar, this can be done by chopping together the ingredients on a large board.

Peel the remaining 3 tomatoes by cutting a shallow cross just through the skin at the bottom, briefly submerging them in boiling water and then transferring them to a bowl of iced water.

Peel off the tomato skins and cut them in half, then scoop out the seeds. Add the tomatoes to the mortar or chopping board and pound or chop to form a paste.

Strain the stock into another large pan, add the sea salad or fresh seaweed and continue to simmer.

Heat the remaining olive oil over a low heat in a large flat-based frying pan or a paella pan, if you happen to have one. Dice the remaining onion, add it to the oil and cook over a low heat for 15 minutes, until softened but not brown.

Bring the stock to a slow boil and poach the fillets of fish, the shrimp and the remaining mussels in it for 5 minutes, until just cooked. Remove with a slotted spoon and set aside.

Serves 4

2kg/4½lb mixed whole fish, such as hake, bream, bass or gurnard (preferably not mackerel or other oily fish)

16 mussels, cleaned and debearded

1 onion, peeled

15ml/1 tbsp mixed seaweed flakes

1 bay leaf

4 garlic cloves, peeled

a pinch of paprika

4 medium tomatoes

1.5 litres/2½ pints/6¼ cups water

120ml/4fl oz/½ cup white wine

a pinch of salt

45ml/3 tbsp olive oil

10g/¼oz dried sea salad or 40g/1½oz fresh dulse, nori or sea greens, shredded

8 large shrimp or prawns, unpeeled

6 saffron threads

475ml/16fl oz/2 cups paella rice

a handful of flat leaf parsley, roughly chopped

lemon wedges, to serve

Add the garlic and paprika mixture to the onion, stir well, and cook down for 2 minutes. Add the saffron and 900ml/1½ pints/3¾ cups of the hot stock, then add the rice, spread it evenly and cook over a low heat for about 20 minutes, until it has absorbed the stock.

Top with the pre-cooked seafood, discarding any mussels that are still closed, and garnish with freshly chopped parsley and lemon wedges.

Variation
If you've purchased pre-prepared fish, use a good-quality bought fish stock to add flavour.

HAKE & KELP SALTIMBOCCA

This is a great recipe for pescetarians, who normally cannot enjoy the classic saltimbocca, in which fish is wrapped in veal or at least pancetta. Using kelp instead of meat infuses the fish with the seaweed's rich umami flavour and creates a soft, delicate texture as the fish steams inside the leaves.

Serves 4

juice of 1 lemon

a trickle of olive oil

5ml/1 tsp sea salad (optional)

a small bunch of thyme, leaves stripped

1 garlic clove, peeled and crushed

seaweed salt and ground pepper, to taste

4 hake fillets

4–6 strips dried or fresh kelp

Combine the lemon juice, oil, sea salad (if using), thyme leaves, garlic and seasoning in a shallow dish, and marinate the fish in it for about an hour.

Place the strips of kelp in a shallow tray, ideally a baking tray, and just cover with water. Leave to soak for about 20 minutes; ideally a gel should form on the outside of the kelp, giving it the texture of pancetta or bacon.

Preheat the oven to 180°C/350°F/Gas 4.

Wrap each piece of fish in kelp, using as many strips as necessary to encase the fish. These can be secured using cocktail sticks or toothpicks.

Place the wrapped fish on a lightly oiled baking tray and roast for 15–20 minutes, until the kelp has become crunchy and the fish is tender inside.

Serve immediately.

SEA SPAGHETTI 'TAGLIATELLE' WITH CRAB

This is a nourishing, simple and quick gluten-free dish of land- and sea-vegetable 'tagliatelle' served with scrumptious crab. This is one of the healthiest seafoods available, and brown crab, along with many other types, is on the MSC sustainable list. Buying it fresh and doing the hard work yourself makes it a really affordable option, but you can use dressed crab or even good-quality frozen or canned crab when the fresh type is not in season.

If using dried sea spaghetti, rehydrate it for 10 minutes in cold water, then drain. Cut either kind into lengths of about 10cm/4in.

Thinly slice the carrot, courgette and leek into ribbons or use a julienne to make them into a 'tagliatelle'. Dice the tomatoes.

Slice the lemon in half lengthways. Reserve half for squeezing. Cut away the skin and pith from the remaining half, then slice the flesh into slender lemon segments.

Heat the oil in a frying pan over a medium heat, then add the garlic, chilli, tomato and crab meat and cook together into a paste for 5 minutes.

Add the vegetable tagliatelle and the seaweed with 250ml/8fl oz/1 cup water and the juice from the reserved lemon half. Stir-fry for 5 minutes, then add pepper to taste.

Garnish with a sprinkling of flaked sea salad and arrange the lemon pieces on top.

Cook's tip
If you want to ensure really tender sea spaghetti you can boil the dried sea spaghetti for 8–10 minutes in a pan of water. This makes the seaweed more tender especially if it is more mature.

Serves 2

50g/2oz fresh sea spaghetti or 15g/½oz dried sea spaghetti
1 carrot, peeled
1 courgette (zucchini)
1 leek
2 tomatoes (canned are fine)
1 lemon
15ml/1 tbsp olive oil
1 garlic clove, peeled and crushed
½ fresh chilli, finely chopped or 2.5ml/½ tsp chilli paste
600g/1lb 6oz crab meat
ground black pepper, to taste
flaked sea salad, to garnish

BAKED OYSTER GRATIN

This baked oyster treat makes eating oysters more accessible; cooking them means they lose the slimy texture that puts off so many people and their texture instead becomes meaty, reminiscent of large mussels. When removing the oysters from the shell use a very sharp knife (take great care) to ensure you cut off the muscle that holds the bivalve closed and include this in the dish – they are deliciously sweet and also add an extra texture.

Preheat the oven to 200°C/400°F/Gas 6.

If using dried sea spaghetti place it in a pan of water and boil it for 8–10 minutes or until tender. Finely chop and set aside.

Discard any oysters that don't close when tapped. Shuck the oysters, ideally with a specialist shucking knife but you can also use a flat-headed screwdriver. Hold the oyster in an old dish towel or rag over a large bowl to catch any spilled juices, and hinge open the shell carefully, trying to retain as much of the juice in the shell as possible.

Discard the top part of the shell and any fragments that may have fallen on the oyster, then place the oysters in their shells into a heatproof dish.

Check the spilled juices for any fragments of shell and remove them, then add the rest of the ingredients and mix well, ensuring the olive oil coats all the bread and the cheese is evenly distributed.

Distribute the gratin topping evenly among the oysters and bake for 15 minutes, until the topping is golden.

Serve with lemon wedges and a tomato and onion salad, if you like.

Serves 4

40g/1½oz fresh sea spaghetti, finely chopped, or 10g/¼oz dried sea spaghetti
24 fresh oysters
6cm-/2½in-thick slices of baguette, cut into small pieces
1 large tomato, diced
1 large garlic clove, peeled and finely chopped
45ml/3 tbsp extra virgin olive oil
125g/4¼oz Camembert, finely chopped
a small handful of fresh fennel, finely chopped
salt and ground black pepper, to taste
lemon wedges and a tomato and onion salad, to serve

SEA GREENS TEMPURA CUTTLEFISH

Sea greens provide the seasoning and boost the fishy flavour of the cuttlefish in this tasty snack, which should be eaten piping hot, while the batter is crunchy. Don't be tempted to use fresh sea greens in the batter, since it will release water as it cooks and spoil the batter. Cuttlefish is sometimes available from fishmongers, but if you can't source any then you can substitute squid rings; pieces of hake, coley, gurnard, salmon or other meaty fish; strips of chicken breast fillet; small chunks of vegetables such as pepper, courgette, cauliflower, broccoli or mushrooms; or even oysters if you're feeling lavish.

First, make the tempura batter. In a bowl, combine the flour with the cornflour, sea greens or sea salad, salt and pepper. Make a well in the middle, then pour in the sparkling water and mix with a fork, until combined. Do this as gently as possible to avoid knocking air out of the batter. The batter should be the consistency of fairly thick custard and should thoroughly coat the cuttlefish. If it is too thick, add a drop more water.

Put the plain flour in a shallow dish and stir in the seasoning. Add the cuttlefish to the flour and toss gently, ensuring each piece is fully coated. Line a serving plate with a piece of kitchen paper.

Pour the oil into a deep, heavy pan suitable for deep-frying and place it over a medium-high heat until it just starts to bubble. To test whether or not the oil is up to temperature, add a small piece of floured cuttlefish or a drop of the batter. When this quickly rises to the surface and sizzles, the oil is at the correct temperature.

Working methodically, dip each piece of floured cuttlefish in the batter to coat thoroughly, then carefully lower this into the hot oil. Do not overcrowd the pan; you will need to cook the cuttlefish in several batches.

Fry each piece for 45–60 seconds, until golden brown, then carefully use a slotted spoon to transfer the cuttlefish to the kitchen paper to drain. Repeat the process until all of the cuttlefish is cooked. Serve immediately with a light aioli and lemon wedges, garnished with sea greens.

Serves 2–4

115g/4oz/1 cup plain (all-purpose) flour

a pinch of salt and ground black pepper

600g/1lb 6oz cuttlefish, cleaned and cut into long strips about 1–2cm/½–¾in wide

rapeseed or vegetable oil, for deep-frying (see Cook's tips)

aioli and lemon wedges, to serve

fresh or dried sea greens, to garnish

For the tempura batter

250g/9oz/generous 2 cups self-raising (self-rising) flour

15ml/1 tbsp cornflour (cornstarch)

30ml/2 tbsp dried sea greens, finely chopped, or sea salad flakes

a pinch of salt and ground black pepper

300ml/½ pint/1¼ cups chilled sparkling water

Cook's tips
- Cuttlefish needs to be cooked in a similar way to squid, ie over a high heat and very quickly, although it's generally slightly more substantial than its cephalopod cousin and does take an extra 20 seconds or so to cook. If using squid, cook it for 30–40 seconds. Be sure not to overcook either type or it will become quite tough.
- Rapeseed oil burns at a higher temperature and is generally free of GM ingredients, unlike many vegetable oils. By running it through a strainer back into its bottle you can happily reuse the oil several times for economy.

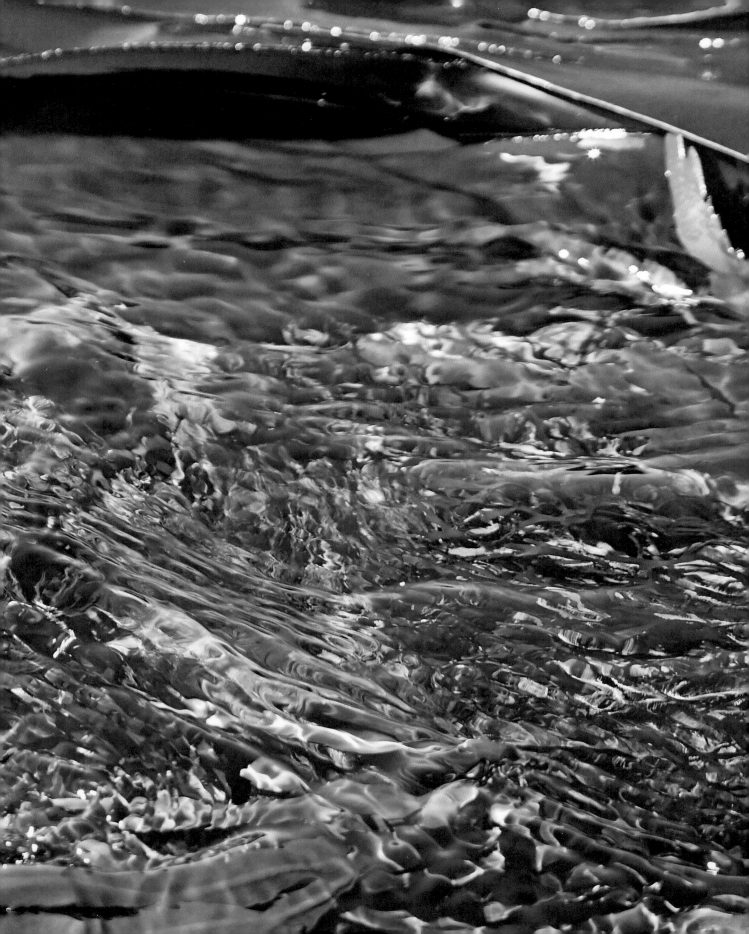

A PLETHORA OF PASTIES

There are many schools of thoughts and arguments had over the art form that is the traditional Cornish pasty, and there are even more types of mass-produced, sludge-filled, plastic-wrapped poor imitations on the market. So let's be clear: here we are speaking only of the heartily filled and lovingly crimped steaming golden packages of joy to be found in village stores, pubs, cafés and speciality outlets. Some say it is the rough-puff pastry made of white flour that is the vital component for a good pasty – but this is not necessarily true; there are delicious pasties made with puff, shortcrust, rough-puff and even vegan spelt pastry. The key is making sure that the filling complements the pastry used (for example, a vegan spelt pastry would not be ideal with a dry filling, but is delicious packed with spicy tomatoes and pulses) and consideration must be given to where the pasty will be eaten and what it will be eaten with. For the average 'on-the-go' pasty-eater, we generally recommend a good rough-puff pastry, which is a deliciously buttery and flaky happy medium between shortcrust and puff.

For the pastry (makes enough for 4 pasties)

450g/1lb/4 cups plain (all-purpose) flour
a pinch of salt
300g/11oz/1½ cups butter
100ml/3½fl oz/scant ½ cup ice-cold water

The trick to keeping your pastry flaky is to handle it as little as possible and to keep your hands and surfaces cold. A glass or marble surface will help with this.

Sift the flour into a mixing bowl and stir in the salt. Grate the butter into the bowl and mix well with the edge of a blunt knife. You are aiming for an uneven breadcrumb consistency for rough puff (if you prefer shortcrust, use your fingertips to rub the butter and flour together and achieve an even breadcrumb texture).

FOR THE ROUGH-PUFF PASTRY:

Add a small quantity of water and mix well with the blunt knife or your fingertips; remember, you are trying to handle it as little as possible. If you prefer to use a food processor, keep it on its slowest setting and do not over-mix.

Keep very gradually adding the water and stirring until the pastry comes together.

Place the dough on a lightly floured surface, then roll it out using a floured rolling pin to form a neat rectangle. Refrigerate it for an hour while you prepare the filling.

Once you have prepared your filling of choice, roll out the chilled pastry on a well-floured surface, keeping a neat rectangular shape by regularly changing the direction in which you roll. You should see streaks of butter – this is what makes the pastry so light and flaky.

When the pastry is evenly rolled to a thickness of 5mm/¼in, fold it in on itself alternating from left to right and top to bottom. Roll out and repeat. Chill for 30 minutes before using.

continued overleaf...

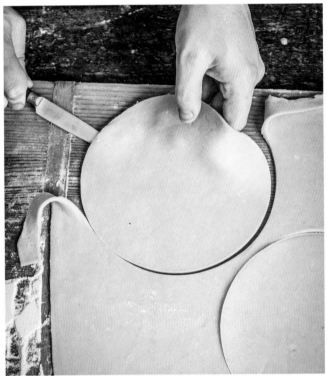

TO MAKE THE PASTIES:

Preheat the oven to 180°C/350°F/Gas 4. Roll out the pastry to a thickness of about 5mm/¼in and cut out four circles, using an average-size dinner plate as a template.

Spoon one-quarter of the filling mixture on to one side of the pastry, leaving a good 3cm/1¼in gap all round for the crimp.

Beat 1 egg with 15ml/1 tbsp milk to make an egg wash and, using a pastry brush, draw a light semi-circle around the outside of the filling.

Fold over the pastry, gently cupping and compacting the filling so that the back edge of the pastry disc meets the egg-washed edge.

Gently push the edges together, then brush the crescent edge with some egg wash.

Starting from the left, take the joined edges with your right thumb below and the index finger above and gently pull the pastry towards you, rotating the finger and thumb so the thumb is on top, gently pushing the crust in on itself. You should now have a knobbly bit on the end.

Keep moving around the pasty repeating this motion. Don't worry if the first couple look a bit messy; after a bit of practice you will quickly get the hang of it. So long as you've kept the pastry intact the filling will stay inside and once it's cooked you'll hardly notice the wobbly edges.

Make a few small slits along the top of the pasties to allow the steam to escape, then place them on one or two baking sheets lined with baking parchment and bake for 45–55 minutes, until golden brown.

Remove from the oven and wait about 10 minutes before eating them.

continued overleaf...

FOR THE FILLINGS:

Cornish pasties are traditionally made using raw ingredients, which comes as a surprise to many. Consider, however, that the pasty will be in the oven for at least half an hour, so as long as the fillings are chopped small enough there will be no problem with them cooking through. For most of the recipes here, simply mix together the ingredients, season well, place on the pastry circles and get crimping. Each of the variations makes four good-size pasties. Tuck in!

Mackerel, horseradish and sea greens

200g/7oz fresh mackerel fillets, cut into 1–2cm/½–¾in chunks
15ml/1 tbsp horseradish sauce or 2.5cm/1in piece of fresh horseradish, finely grated
1 large potato, peeled and diced into 5mm/¼in cubes
6 spring onions (scallions), roughly chopped
50g/2oz fresh sea greens or 10g/¼oz dried sea greens, finely chopped
a squeeze of lemon
salt and ground black pepper

Liver, dulse and mushroom

150g/5oz liver, diced
50g/2oz fresh dulse, finely chopped, or 10g/¼oz flaked dulse
50g/2oz mushrooms, sliced and sautéed in butter with garlic, seasoned, then left to cool
1 medium onion, peeled and diced
1 large potato, peeled and diced
salt and ground black pepper

continued overleaf...

Mushroom, capers and sea spaghetti

Pork, apple and dulse

100g/3¾oz button (white) or chestnut mushrooms, sliced and sautéed in butter with garlic, seasoned, then left to cool	150g/5oz pork fillet (tenderloin), diced
30ml/2 tbsp drained capers	2 apples, peeled and diced
50g/2oz fresh sea spaghetti or 15g/½oz dried sea spaghetti, rehydrated in cold water for 10 minutes, chopped into 2–3cm/¾–1¼in lengths	1.25ml/¼ tsp fresh thyme leaves or a good pinch of dried thyme
	50g/2oz fresh dulse, finely chopped, or 10g/¼oz flaked dulse
1 medium onion, peeled and diced	1 medium onion, peeled and diced
1 large potato, peeled and diced	1 large potato, peeled and diced
salt and ground black pepper	salt and ground black pepper

Stilton, walnut and sea spaghetti

150g/5oz Stilton, or similar hard blue cheese, crumbled

100g/3¾oz walnuts, roughly chopped

50g/2oz fresh sea spaghetti or 15g/½oz dried sea spaghetti, rehydrated in cold water for 10 minutes, chopped into 2–3cm/¾–1¼in lengths

1 medium onion, peeled and diced

1 large potato, peeled and diced

salt and ground black pepper

Cheese, onion and sea salad

300g/11oz/scant 3 cups grated mature (sharp) Cheddar cheese

200g/7oz swede (rutabaga), peeled and diced

2 medium onions, peeled and diced

1 large potato, peeled and diced

90ml/6 tbsp fresh sea salad, or 15g/½oz dried sea salad, finely chopped

salt and ground black pepper

15ml/1 tbsp wholegrain mustard (optional)

CHICKEN, MUSHROOM & SEA SPAGHETTI PIE

This is a really simple, sustaining and delicious pie that can be made from scratch with chicken breast fillets or with leftover roast chicken. Sea spaghetti brings taste and texture to the party.

Serves 4–6

30ml/2 tbsp olive oil
3 skinless, boneless chicken breast fillets or about 500g/1¼lb cooked chicken, cut into bitesize chunks
250g/9oz mushrooms, roughly chopped
1 onion, peeled and finely chopped
2 garlic cloves, peeled and finely chopped
a small handful of fresh thyme sprigs, leaves picked
30ml/2 tbsp plain (all-purpose) flour
400ml/14fl oz/1⅔ cups hot chicken stock
200ml/7fl oz/scant 1 cup hot milk
a pinch of salt
freshly ground white pepper
50g/2oz fresh sea spaghetti or 15g/½oz dried sea spaghetti, chopped into 2–3cm/¾–1¼in lengths
30ml/2 tbsp parsley
30ml/2 tbsp chives
500g/1¼lb puff pastry (or use rough-puff pastry, see page 177)
1 egg, beaten
steamed vegetables, to serve

Heat half the oil in a large pan over a medium heat, then add the raw chicken, if using. When the chicken starts to turn white, add the mushrooms and cook for about 10 minutes or until golden brown.

Transfer the chicken and mushrooms to a bowl and set aside. If using pre-cooked chicken, stir it into the mushrooms. Add the remaining oil to the same pan and sweat the onion and garlic in it for about 10 minutes, until softened. Add the picked thyme leaves.

Add the flour and cook for 1 minute, stirring continuously. Remove the pan from the heat and slowly whisk in first the stock, then the milk, and whisk until smooth. Season, then stir in the sea spaghetti and the chicken and mushroom mixture.

Return to the heat and bring to the boil. Reduce to a simmer and cook for 25 minutes or until the sauce has thickened. Remove from the heat and stir in the parsley and chives, then spoon into a medium-size pie dish with a lip and leave to cool. Preheat the oven to 200°C/400°F/Gas 6. Roll out the pasty on a floured surface to a thickness of 5mm/¼in.

Brush a little of the beaten egg around the rim of the pie dish. Cut a long, thin strip of pastry to fit around the rim and push it down into place. Gently lift the sheet of pastry on to the pie, pressing lightly at the edges to secure it in place. Trim any excess pastry with a sharp knife. Brush the top of the pastry with more beaten egg.

Place the pie on a baking sheet to catch any spills and bake for 30 minutes or until the pastry has risen and turned a beautiful dark golden-brown colour. Serve with steamed vegetables.

SEA SPAGHETTI, BEEF & GUINNESS PIE

Steak and ale pie is an all-time classic, but here it is given a seaweed twist with the addition of sea spaghetti as well as the often-forgotten oysters that were once widely used to lend cheap substance to dishes such as this. The ozone tang and added textural interest these two ingredients introduce elevate this from standard pub grub to foodie fantasy, all topped off with a golden cap of home-made rough-puff pastry.

Serves 4–6

30ml/2 tbsp plain (all-purpose) flour
a pinch of black pepper and salt
700g/1lb 9oz stewing beef, cubed
30ml/2 tbsp sunflower oil
225g/8oz mushrooms, chopped
1 onion, peeled and chopped
50g/2oz fresh sea spaghetti or 15g/½oz dried sea spaghetti, rehydrated in cold water for 10 minutes, chopped into 2–3cm/¾–1¼in lengths
6–8 oysters, shucked and strained, juice reserved (see page 171)
425ml/15fl oz/1¾ cups Guinness or other dry stout
15ml/1 tbsp Worcestershire sauce
200g/7oz rough-puff pastry (see page 177)
beaten egg, to glaze
steamed vegetables, to serve

Combine the flour and seasoning in a bowl, then add the beef and toss to coat.

Heat the oil in a large pan over a high heat, then add the beef cubes a few at a time and seal and brown all over. Do this in batches and take care not to overcrowd the pan or the beef will boil rather than caramelise. Set aside.

Fry the mushrooms and onion in the same pan, adding a little extra oil if necessary, for about 10 minutes, until soft. Stir in the beef.

Stir in the sea spaghetti, oyster juice, Guinness and Worcestershire sauce. Cover and cook over a low heat for about 1½ hours, until the beef is tender. Set aside and leave to cool before adding the oysters.

Preheat the oven to 200°C/400°F/Gas 6. Roll out the pasty on a floured surface to a thickness of 5mm/¼in.

Pour the mixture into a greased pie dish, then brush the edge with a little beaten egg. Gently lift the sheet of pastry on to the pie, leaving a slight overhang.

Crimp firmly, brush the top with beaten egg, then cut a hole in the middle. You could also lightly score the surface of the pastry into small diamonds using a very sharp knife.

Place the pie on a baking sheet to catch any drips and bake for 15 minutes. Reduce the heat to 180°C/350°F/Gas 4 and bake for 30 minutes more.

Serve immediately with some steamed vegetables.

KELP LASAGNE TWO WAYS

The layers of kelp in this dish give an added depth to the flavours and a new texture, alongside the more familiar lasagne sheets. There are two versions here: one vegetarian and one made with beef. If making the vegetarian one, use vegetarian cheese if appropriate.

First, make the béchamel sauce. Gently melt the butter in a heavy pan, then stir in the flour to make a roux. Stir on a very low heat to cook out the flour for 1–2 minutes.

Pour in the wine if using and allow the alcohol to cook off for a few seconds before gradually pouring in the milk, stirring constantly with a whisk until a smooth, creamy texture is reached. Add the mustard powder and seasoning.

To make the vegetarian filling, preheat the oven to 200°C/400°F/Gas 6. Put the aubergine, onion and pepper in a roasting pan and trickle over olive oil to coat. Season, stir to combine, then spread out the vegetables in a single layer. Roast for 30 minutes, stirring once.

Meanwhile, heat about 15ml/1 tbsp olive oil in a small pan over a medium heat. Once the oil is hot enough that a little garlic sizzles immediately upon contact with it, add all of the garlic and cook until golden brown, stirring frequently to prevent it from burning. Add the passata and the basil or pesto and season to taste.

Once the roasted vegetables are done, pour over the tomato sauce and stir well.

...continued overleaf

Serves 4–6

115g/4oz fresh kelp or 30g/1½oz dried kelp, rehydrated in water for 20 minutes
about 115g/4oz lasagne sheets
filling of your choice, see below
olive oil, for greasing
45ml/3 tbsp grated Parmesan cheese
a sprinkle of paprika
a sprinkle of Mediterranean herbs

For the béchamel sauce

115g/4oz/½ cup butter
115g/4oz/1 cup plain (all-purpose) flour
a splash of white wine (optional)
900ml/1½ pints/3¾ cups hot whole (full-fat) milk (or oat, goat, rice or soya milk, if preferred)
5ml/1 tsp mustard powder
salt and ground black pepper, to taste

For the vegetarian filling

1 large aubergine (eggplant), diced into 1cm/½in pieces
1 onion, peeled and diced into 1cm/½in pieces
1 red (bell) pepper, seeded and diced into 1cm/½in pieces
olive oil
2 garlic cloves, peeled and finely chopped
200ml/7fl oz/scant 1 cup passata (bottled strained tomatoes)
a bunch of fresh basil leaves, shredded or 15ml/1 tbsp green pesto
salt and ground black pepper

Cook's tip
Try skipping the lasagne sheets entirely and using only kelp sheets. This is a wonderful gluten-free alternative if you use buckwheat instead of regular flour too!

For the beef filling

15ml/1 tbsp olive oil

1 onion, peeled and finely chopped

a splash of red wine (optional)

2 garlic cloves, peeled and finely chopped or crushed

200g/7oz good-quality minced (ground) beef

salt and ground black pepper

1 large carrot, peeled and grated

400g/14oz can chopped tomatoes

1 beef stock (bouillon) cube

a handful of fresh oregano leaves, shredded or 2.5ml/
½ tsp dried oregano

To make the beef filling, heat the olive oil in a large pan over a medium heat, add the onion and fry for about 10 minutes, or until softened and golden brown. Pour in the red wine, if using, and sizzle to reduce the alcohol.

Add the garlic, beef and seasoning and mix well to combine. Cook, stirring frequently, until the meat is cooked through, then add the grated carrot and chopped tomatoes.

Half fill the can with water and swill it around, then add the liquid to the pan along with the stock cube. Simmer for 30 minutes, until reduced and intense in flavour. Finally, add the herbs and taste to check the seasoning.

TO MAKE THE LASAGNE:

Preheat the oven to 180°C/350°F/Gas 4 (or reduce the heat if you made the vegetarian filling). To assemble the lasagne, grease an appropriate dish with olive oil and spoon one-third of the béchamel sauce into the bottom to form a layer. Cover with a layer of kelp and gently spoon in a layer of the vegetable or beef filling, using about half of the mixture.

Place a layer of lasagne sheets over the top and then pour on a layer of béchamel sauce. Now for a layer of kelp, followed by the final layer of the filling mixture. Place the final layer of lasagne sheets on top, then spread over the remainder of the béchamel sauce.

Top with grated Parmesan, paprika and Mediterranean herbs and place the dish on a baking sheet to catch any drips. Bake for 30–40 minutes, until golden and bubbling. Remove from the oven and allow to sit for 10 minutes before serving – this helps the layers hold together.

Chapter 4
SALADS & DIPS

Just when you thought salad couldn't get any healthier, along comes seaweed and elevates your greenery to a whole new level! What's more, you don't have to wait until summer to use these beautifully fresh recipes – their vibrant colours and textures can be enjoyed at any time of the year, come rain or shine. We enjoy sharing them straight out the bowl on the beach but they look fantastic on the table, too, as part of a feast or even as the main meal event when combined with hearty fare such as fish, shellfish, cheese or grains.

And what better accompaniment than a range of tasty dips? Here, we've given a seaside slant to much-loved classics such as pesto, hummus and raita, as well as sauces and salad dressing.

So whatever the weather and no matter where you are, inject a little Vitamin Sea into your meals and set your tastebuds a-tingle.

SEA SPAGHETTI WEST-COUNTRY SALAD

Farmer's markets are excellent places in which to pick up regional and locally produced foods. The ingredients for this salad are local to Cornwall, in the south-west of the UK, but you can swap in whatever similar ingredients are available according to where you are and the season. If you can't make it to a market, the ingredients are also readily available at supermarkets. A meal in itself, this tasty, simple salad is especially good for brunch at the weekend, the strands of sea spaghetti seasoning and enhancing the various component parts.

Cook the new potatoes and dried sea spaghetti, if using, in a pan of boiling water for 10–15 minutes or steam them for about 20 minutes, until cooked through. Drain, if necessary, and leave to cool.

Slice the potatoes lengthways into slices about 5mm/¼in in thickness. Place these in a bowl and toss with the olive oil and a little salt and pepper.

Heat the butter in the frying pan over a medium heat, then add the slices of potato and fry for about 10 minutes, turning them gently halfway through the cooking time, until golden all over.

Add the sea spaghetti and mushrooms and cook for about 5 minutes. Add the crushed garlic and cook for a further 2–3 minutes, until the mushrooms are soft and golden and the garlic is just slightly softened. Remove the pan from the heat and cover it with foil to keep everything warm.

Bring a pan of lightly salted water to the boil, then reduce the heat until the water is just simmering. Carefully crack in the eggs and poach them for about 3 minutes, until they are cooked but still soft in the middles.

Meanwhile, add the lemon juice and chopped parsley to the potato mixture and shave the cheese into it using a vegetable peeler. Season to taste and gently stir to combine.

Divide the potato mixture between four plates and top each portion with a poached egg. Arrange the parsley sprigs on top and serve and serve immediately.

Serves 4

200g/7oz new potatoes
75g/3oz fresh sea spaghetti or 10g/¼oz dried sea spaghetti (fresh is preferable, if possible)
a drizzle of olive oil
seaweed salt and ground black pepper, to taste
a pat of butter
200g/7oz field or portobello mushrooms, wiped clean and sliced
3 garlic cloves, peeled and crushed
4 eggs
juice of 1 lemon
15ml/1 tbsp chopped parsley, plus some sprigs, to garnish
200g/7oz strong (ideally West Country) Cheddar cheese

QUINOA, SEA SALAD, GRILLED HALLOUMI & POMEGRANATE SALAD

This superfood-packed salad sings with colour and flavour, and is a doddle to throw together, meaning you don't have to spend hours in the kitchen to produce something delicious and healthy. The little pink pomegranate nuggets add a lovely sweetness to this dish and perfectly complement the saltiness of the halloumi and the umami tang of the sea salad.

Rinse the quinoa well, then place it in a pan with plenty of cold water and a pinch of salt. Bring to the boil, then simmer for about 12 minutes. The quinoa is cooked when the grains are tender but retain a nutty bite and the kernels are coming away from the seeds. Drain in a fine strainer and set aside, allowing the quinoa to steam to reduce the moisture.

Sprinkle both sides of the halloumi slices with a pinch of paprika. Heat about 15ml/1 tbsp of the olive oil in a frying pan over a medium heat, then add the sliced halloumi and cook for 3 minutes, until the underside is golden.

Gently turn over the slices with a fish slice and cook the other side for 3 minutes. Do not move the slices around while they are cooking or they may break up. Remove from the pan and cut into 1cm-/½in-wide strips.

Roll the pomegranate on a hard surface to loosen the seeds then slice it in half, turn it inside out over a large bowl (to catch the juices) and pop out the individual segments. A faster, but messier, method is to hold the half cut side down over the bowl and tap the skin with a wooden spoon, squeezing a little to release the seeds. Be warned: this may cause juice to splatter, which can stain clothing.

Add the quinoa, herbs, seaweed, remaining 15ml/ 1 tbsp olive oil and lime juice to the bowl of pomegranate seeds, season to taste and stir to combine.

Divide the quinoa mixture between four plates and top with a few slices of the halloumi, or pile all of the quinoa on to a serving dish and top with all of the halloumi so that diners can help themselves.

Serves 4 as a main or 8 as a side dish

200g/7oz/generous 1 cup quinoa

salt and ground black pepper, to taste

100g/3¾oz halloumi, cut into 5mm-/¼in-thick slices

30ml/2 tbsp olive oil

a pinch of paprika

1 ripe pomegranate

a few sprigs of tarragon (or basil, if you prefer), shredded

30ml/2 tbsp dried sea salad flakes or a few sprigs of fresh nori, dulse or sea greens, finely chopped

a squeeze of fresh lime

Cook's tip

Quinoa (pronounced keen wah) is a Latin American seed that has become increasingly popular over the last decade. High in protein and packed with goodness, it makes a great alternative to rice or couscous.

THAI CRAB, MANGO & SEA SALAD

This luxurious combination of fresh, sweet, juicy mango and delectable crab is given a colour, flavour and nutritional boost by the addition of a little sea salad. Fresh crab is best when it is in season, although you could use good-quality canned crab if necessary.

Serves 2

2 bundles of vermicelli rice noodles

1 firm mango

1 red onion

500g/1¼lb white crab meat

1 fresh chilli, sliced

1 garlic clove, peeled and crushed

15ml/1 tbsp dried sea salad flakes or a few sprigs of fresh nori, dulse or sea greens, finely chopped

juice of 1 lime

15–30ml/1–2 tbsp olive oil, or to taste

30–45ml/2–3 tbsp roughly chopped fresh coriander (cilantro)

a pinch of salt

'Cook' or rehydrate the vermicelli rice noodles according to the packet instructions, then cut them into pieces measuring about 5cm/2in in length.

Peel the mango, then grate it and put it in a large mixing bowl, along with its juices.

Peel the onion, them cut in half vertically and slice each half into thin crescent-shaped slices.

Add the onion to the mango, along with the crab, noodles, chilli, garlic and half of the seaweed and gently combine.

Add the lime juice, olive oil and half of the chopped fresh coriander and give everything a good mix. Taste and season with salt as required.

Serve garnished with the remaining chopped coriander and flaked or fresh seaweed.

TUNA, BEAN & SEA SALAD

This is a lovely, fresh summer salad that uses both fresh and canned beans and takes only about 15 minutes to make. The sea salad flakes lift the flavour of the tuna and beans, as well as giving the dish an additional health boost. A complete meal in one, this is ideal picnic fare since the flavours only improve over time – just keep it cool while carrying it around.

Bring a small volume of water to the boil in a pan. Add the green beans and cook for 4 minutes, until just soft, then drain and immediately rinse in cold water to stop the cooking and fix the lovely green colour.

Make the dressing by whisking together all of the ingredients in a large bowl. If using seaweed or kelp flakes, set aside for 1 hour for the flavours to mingle.

Add all the beans to the bowl, along with the tomatoes, spring onions, seaweed and fresh coriander and mix it all together gently, using a folding action. Ensure that the beans are completely coated in the dressing.

Flake the tuna over the top and drizzle over a little olive oil. Season to taste, and serve whenever you are ready to.

Serves 4

200g/7oz green beans, trimmed and halved

400g/14oz canned butter (lima) beans, rinsed and drained

400g/14oz canned red kidney beans, rinsed and drained

4 large tomatoes, chopped

2 spring onions (scallions), chopped

15ml/1 tbsp dried sea salad flakes or a few sprigs of fresh nori, dulse or sea greens, finely chopped

a handful of chopped fresh coriander (cilantro)

about 350g/12oz canned sustainable tuna, drained if necessary

a drizzle of olive oil

salt and ground black pepper, to taste

For the dressing

15ml/1 tbsp extra virgin olive oil

5ml/1 tsp cider vinegar

5ml/1 tsp mustard seeds or mustard

1 garlic clove, peeled and crushed

2.5ml/½ tsp mixed seaweed or kelp flakes (optional)

salt and ground black pepper

CAULIFLOWER, MUSHROOM, DULSE & TARRAGON 'RICE'

The popularity of recipes that cut out grains and pulses has grown in tandem with the increasing numbers of people suffering from food allergies or intolerances. Accompaniments such as cauliflower or broccoli 'rice' are being embraced by those who don't suffer from intolerances, too, providing a tasty and easy way to up the daily vegetable intake. This jazzed-up cauliflower 'rice' bulked out with mushrooms and tender strips of dulse takes very little time to prepare and is delicious both cold and hot.

Serves 4 as an accompaniment

1 cauliflower, cut into small chunks

30ml/2 tbsp butter or olive oil

12 button (white) mushrooms, wiped clean and quartered

2 garlic cloves, peeled and chopped

10g/¼oz fresh dulse or 5g/⅛oz dried dulse, soaked for 5 minutes in just enough water to be absorbed, chopped into 2.5cm-/1in-long pieces

salt and ground black pepper (or pepper dulse)

a small bunch of fresh tarragon, finely chopped

Cook's tip

Mushrooms release a lot of their water if you add salt too early, resulting in slimy grey things, reminiscent of canned mushrooms. For this reason it is best to cook them until they are golden brown before seasoning.

Put the cauliflower pieces in a food processor and blitz until it forms grains about the same size as rice or couscous. Set aside.

Heat half the butter or olive oil in a frying pan, then add the quartered mushrooms and cook for about 5 minutes, until golden brown.

Add the garlic and dulse and season well. Cook for a couple more minutes, until the garlic is cooked, then remove from the heat and set aside.

In a separate large pan with a lid, warm the remaining butter or oil, then add the cauliflower and a pinch of salt. Cook on a low heat for 4–5 minutes, stirring occasionally, until the cauliflower is tender (it's delicious raw so don't worry about undercooking it – it's overcooking you need to watch out for).

Add the mushrooms, sprinkle over the chopped tarragon, stir well and serve.

SPICY BEETROOT, SEA SALAD & SESAME SALAD

Simple, quick and delicious, this phytonutrient-rich side dish is perfect served with Sea Salad Hummus (see page 215) and pitta for a colourful and nutritious lunch. The easiest (and least messy) way to grate the beetroot is to peel it and then grate it in a food processor fitted with a shredding blade. These vibrant little strips are then partially 'cooked' by the acid of the vinegar, which softens them at the same time as complementing their slightly sweet, earthy flavour. The vinegar also has many health benefits, meaning this humble little dish really is a powerhouse of goodness.

Toast the sesame seeds in a heavy pan over a very low heat for about 5 minutes, until golden brown and fragrant. Stay with the pan and shake it frequently to prevent the sesame seeds from burning, which makes them bitter and unpleasant to eat. Set aside to cool.

Meanwhile, put the grated beetroot and all the remaining ingredients in a serving bowl and stir to combine.

Leave for about 15 minutes for the vinegar to soften the beetroot and for the flavours to infuse, then sprinkle over the cooled sesame seeds and serve.

Serves 2–4 as an accompaniment

30ml/2 tbsp sesame seeds

2 raw beetroots (beets), peeled and grated

15ml/1 tbsp apple cider vinegar

15ml/1 tbsp toasted sesame oil

1 mild fresh green chilli, seeded and finely diced

15–30ml/1–2 tbsp dried sea salad flakes or a few sprigs of fresh nori, dulse or sea greens, finely chopped

POTATO SALAD

The ubiquitous and infinitely versatile potato salad is given a tangy twist in this recipe
with the addition of a few spoonfuls of yogurt and a sprinkling of sea salad flakes. Use a
waxy variety of potato and try to buy good-quality mayonnaise made with free-range eggs
if possible. Serve it alongside grilled meat or fish or as part of a spread alongside
some roasted vegetables and green salads.

Dry-fry the mustard seeds in a heavy pan over a
medium-high heat for 1–2 minutes, until they start to
pop. Set aside to cool, then briefly grind them in a
pestle and mortar; allow them to keep some texture,
don't crush them to a powder.

Bring a pan of water to the boil, then add the new
potatoes, rosemary and garlic. Boil for 10–15 minutes,
until tender and cooked through, then drain and leave
to cool slightly. Discard the rosemary.

Once the potatoes are just warm, put them into a large
bowl and add all of the other ingredients.

Gently stir to combine well, then cover and leave
for about 30 minutes for the flavours to blend
before serving.

Serves 4 as an accompaniment

5ml/1 tsp mustard seeds
500g/1¼lb new potatoes
a sprig of rosemary
1 garlic clove, peeled and crushed
30–45ml/2–3 tbsp mayonnaise
30ml/2 tbsp natural (plain) yogurt
45ml/3 tbsp spring onions (scallions), thinly sliced
30ml/2 tbsp dried sea salad flakes or a few sprigs of fresh nori, dulse or sea greens, finely chopped
a squeeze of lemon juice
salt and ground black pepper, to taste

Variations

- Using a dash of lemon juice and some yogurt cuts
through the oiliness often associated with this salad,
but if you prefer you could omit these and just use a
little more mayonnaise.

- Use this recipe as a template and experiment by
adding other ingredients. Chopped hard-boiled
egg; chopped capers or cornichons; chopped soft
herbs such as mint, parsley, basil or wild garlic; finely
diced red onion; sliced strands of sea spaghetti…
The list of possibilities is long, so have a go and see
what suits you.

COLESLAW WITH SEA SALAD

This basic coleslaw recipe seasoned with seaweed is delicious as it is, but do feel free to experiment.
Toasted seeds and nuts make a crunchy addition, or spice it up with some chopped fresh chilli,
add sultanas for a sweeter taste, replace all the mayonnaise with thick yogurt, use fresh coriander
and lime for a slightly Thai alternative, or use dill instead of oregano
and serve it with fish. The world is your oyster!

Serves 4 as an accompaniment

½ a medium-sized white cabbage, thinly sliced

3 carrots, peeled and grated

4 spring onions (scallions), thinly sliced

1 small red onion, peeled and thinly sliced

a few sprigs of fresh oregano, leaves picked

a squeeze of lemon juice

30ml/2 tbsp dried sea salad flakes or a few sprigs of fresh nori, dulse or sea greens, finely chopped

90ml/6 tbsp mayonnaise (or swap half for natural (plain) yogurt, if preferred)

salt, to taste

Simply mix all the ingredients together in a large bowl, adding the salt last so that it doesn't start to draw out moisture so quickly from the vegetables, which makes the coleslaw watery.

Cover the coleslaw and leave it to sit for at least a couple of hours, preferably overnight. If you're using toasted nuts or seeds, add these just before serving or they will go soft.

SEAWEED SIDES

In addition to being used as a constituent part of other dishes, seaweed can also be enjoyed as a side dish in its own right. This treatment is especially useful after a successful foraging trip when you have plenty of the fresh green stuff to hand.

Boiled kelp

Put some fresh kelp in a pan of boiling water and cook it for about 30 minutes, until it is softened. It can now be eaten on its own or chopped and used in a range of dishes, such as salads, couscous or rice side dishes, or mixed with other cooked vegetables as a side.

Steamed sea spaghetti with toasted sesame seeds and soy sauce

Steam some fresh sea spaghetti for 10 minutes or until tender. If using dried sea spaghetti it needs to be steamed for 30 minutes or until tender.

Dry-fry 15ml/1 tbsp sesame seeds in a wok or frying pan over a medium heat for a few minutes, stirring frequently, until toasted and golden. Add the cooked sea spaghetti, a drizzle of sesame oil and a splash of soy sauce to the wok or frying pan and mix together.

A PAIR OF PESTOS

Pesto is a staple sauce in many households, transforming a plate of bland pasta into a satisfyingly tasty meal. Store-bought versions are often rather salty and lacking in freshness, so it is well worth whipping up a batch of your own – it takes mere moments and you can tailor the ingredients to exactly suit your palate. Here are a couple of seaweed versions that really ring the changes.

Serves 4–6

To serve

500g/1¼lb cooked penne pasta

15ml/1 tbsp extra virgin olive oil

15 cherry tomatoes, halved (optional)

fresh basil leaves

30ml/2 tbsp flaked dulse or kelp, to garnish

shavings of Parmesan cheese, to serve

For the creamy avocado and dulse pesto

1 ripe avocado

a large bunch (about 40g/1½oz) of fresh basil

30ml/2 tbsp flaked dulse

115g/4oz/1 cup walnuts, lightly toasted

75ml/5 tbsp extra virgin olive oil

1 garlic clove, peeled

seaweed salt and ground pepper, to taste

45ml/3 tbsp lemon juice

For the kelp pesto

50g/2oz/½ cup pine nuts or crushed mixed nuts

100g/3¾oz fresh kelp or 30g/1¼oz dried kelp, soaked in cold water for 20 minutes, finely chopped

65g/2½oz fresh basil

40g/1½oz/½ cup freshly grated Parmesan cheese

5 tbsp/75ml extra virgin olive oil

1 garlic clove, peeled

freshly ground black pepper

Creamy avocado and dulse pesto

This superfood sauce packs a real nutritional punch with the addition of avocado, walnuts and dulse flakes. If you aren't going to eat the pesto immediately, leave out the avocado and mash it in once you are ready to eat. To make the dish gluten- or dairy-free, simply use gluten-free pasta and omit the cheese, as required.

To make the pesto, put all the ingredients into a food processor and pulse until a creamy sauce forms.

Trickle the cooked pasta with olive oil, then stir in the pesto and the tomatoes, if using. Garnish with basil and sprinkle over the dulse flakes, then serve with shavings of Parmesan.

Kelp pesto

This bright-green pesto is more similar to the traditional sauce, but with an extra flavour dimension thanks to the kelp. Test and adjust the quantities as you go to create the ideal balance, but beware adding extra salt since the seaweed lends a briny flavour and Parmesan is fairly salty.

Place the pine nuts or mixed nuts in a dry frying pan over a medium-low heat and toast for a few minutes, shaking often and staying with the pan the whole time. Leave to cool.

Place all the ingredients in a blender or pestle and mortar and blitz or bash until a sauce forms.

Trickle the cooked pasta with olive oil, then stir in the pesto and the tomatoes, if using. Garnish with basil and sprinkle over the dulse flakes, then serve with shavings of Parmesan.

SEA SALAD HUMMUS

Hummus is the go-to dip of choice for many, and it's easy to see why: it's delicious, nourishing and infinitely versatile. This version introduces kelp during the cooking, and specks of sea salad during the processing, producing a perfectly balanced and well-seasoned paste that you will want to make time and again.

If you are using dried chickpeas, soak them overnight in cold water. Drain then place in a pan of fresh water with the kelp and salt. You will need about twice the volume of water as chickpeas. Bring to the boil, turn down to a simmer and cook for about 1 hour or until tender.

When the chickpeas are done, drain them over a bowl and reserve the water, then rinse the chickpeas. They are now ready to use.

Put the cooked or drained canned chickpeas in a blender or food processor with the remaining ingredients and pulse until smooth, adding the water gradually until the desired consistency is reached.

Taste and adjust the seasoning and flavours as required, then serve immediately or store in an airtight container in the refrigerator for up to 3 days. Dust with smoked paprika if you like before serving.

Serves 4–6

115g/4oz/½ cup dried chickpeas or 400g/14oz canned chickpeas in unsalted water, drained
1 large strip of fresh or dried kelp (if using dried chickpeas)
salt
10ml/2 tsp tahini
juice of 1 lemon
60ml/4 tbsp extra virgin olive oil
30ml/2 tbsp dried sea salad flakes or a few sprigs of fresh nori, dulse or sea greens, finely chopped
1–2 garlic cloves, peeled and chopped
a splash of water, if using canned chickpeas (use the cooking water if using dried chickpeas)
smoked paprika, to garnish (optional)

Variations

- Try making a raw version of this classic dip using sprouted chickpeas. Soak the chickpeas overnight, then drain and rinse. Repeat, washing the chickpeas twice daily for 2–4 days, draining them well each time, until the chickpeas have sprouted. This makes a crunchier dip and harnesses the maximum nutritional value of the pulses.
- Use roasted garlic instead of raw.
- Top with caramelised onions (see the Jerusalem artichoke and dulse soup recipe on page 84).
- Top with toasted sesame seeds and dulse.

SEAWEED RAITA/TZATZIKI

This classic accompaniment can be served alongside Sea Salad Hummus (see page 215) as part of a mezze spread, or used as a raita alongside Indian dishes such as Sea Spaghetti Bhajis (see pages 127) Sea Paneer or Tofu (see page 159) or Sea Aloo (see page 144).

Serves 4–6 as an accompaniment

½ cucumber

1 garlic clove

300ml/½ pint/1¼ cups full-fat natural (plain) yogurt

15ml/1 tbsp flaked sea greens

a squeeze of fresh lime or lemon juice (for raita)

a pinch of seaweed salt

a pinch of pepper dulse flakes or ground black pepper

a handful of fresh mint or coriander (cilantro) leaves, chopped

Grate the cucumber into a strainer and push out the excess liquid using the back of a spoon. Pat dry with a piece of kitchen paper, then put it in a serving bowl.

Peel the garlic, then crush it into the cucumber. Add the remaining ingredients and stir well to combine.

Serve immediately, or store, covered, in the refrigerator for up to 24 hours.

SPICY GINGER & KELP SOY

This deeply umami sauce takes minutes to make and will keep well in the refrigerator for several weeks. Try brushing it on chicken before cooking it on a barbecue; using it to marinate shredded cucumber and red pepper; serve it with Sea Salad Oat Cakes (see page 260) and a good strong cheese; or combine it with some sesame oil and serve it with sushi.

Makes 200ml/7fl oz/scant 1 cup

2 x 6cm/2½in strips of fresh kelp or dried kelp, rehydrated in cold water for 20 minutes

1cm/½in piece of fresh root ginger

1 small chilli

200ml/7fl oz/scant 1 cup dark soy sauce

Cut the kelp into short, thin strips.

Peel the ginger, then slice it finely and cut each slice into slender strips.

Slice the chilli lengthways and remove the seeds, then cut it into strips.

Combine all the ingredients and leave to marinate for a few days, or at least overnight.

CAPER, PEPPER DULSE & HORSERADISH SAUCE

This tart little number is ideal for cutting through the oiliness of a battered goujon,
or as a spicy alternative to tartare sauce with your fish and chips.

Serves 4–6

1 shallot, peeled and finely diced

a pinch of ground pepper dulse

45ml/3 tbsp capers

grated rind and juice of 1 lemon

15ml/1 tbsp horseradish sauce or finely grated horseradish
(if available)

200ml/7fl oz/scant 1 cup natural (plain) yogurt (or good-quality
mayonnaise, if preferred)

a pinch of seaweed salt

Peel and dice the shallot and finely chop the pepper
dulse, then place both in a bowl.

Drain then chop the capers and add them to the bowl
along with the lemon rind and juice, horseradish,
yogurt and seaweed salt.

Mix together all of the ingredients and leave for
at least half an hour for the flavours to infuse
before serving.

SEAWEED SALAD DRESSING

There are so many ways to inject a seaweed boost into your daily diet, and adding a little sea salad to your dressing must be one of the easiest.

Mix together the honey, wholegrain mustard and sea green flakes in a bowl.

Gradually pour in the olive oil, whisking continuously, until a fairly thick and even consistency forms, with the mustard grains and seaweed suspended throughout the mixture.

Slowly add the wine and vinegar, whisking continually to emulsify the dressing. If the dressing is thicker than required, you can let it down with a splash of water, again, whisking continually as you add.

If the dressing separates you can always give it a whizz with a hand blender or put it in a bottle or jar and give it a shake before serving.

Makes about 175ml/6fl oz/¾ cup

5ml/1 tsp clear honey

10ml/2 tsp wholegrain mustard

15ml/1 tbsp flaked sea greens

100ml/3½fl oz/scant ½ cup extra virgin olive oil

30ml/2 tbsp dry white wine

30ml/2 tbsp cider vinegar

salt and ground black pepper, to taste

Variation
Try replacing the honey with a splash of elderflower cordial and lemon juice for a summery alternative that is perfect with fish.

Chapter 5
DESSERTS

OK trust us on this one. Seaweed can work really well in desserts. Whether using deep-flavoured dulse to bring out the richness in chocolate or Irish moss as an ethical, vegan alternative to gelatine, seaweed brings a new level of taste to your favourite puddings. It's also super-healthy, which makes indulging in something sweet even more satisfying.

You'll be able to easily taste the seaweed in some of these recipes, to great effect, whereas in others you won't be able to tell it's in there. And for some, the bright colour of certain seaweeds lifts the look of a dish, while in others it remains an invisible, health-boosting sea-cret weapon that works its magic in the background.

So next time you meet friends for dinner, bring along one of these desserts – they never fail to impress and have that extra something special that will create quite a stir.

BAKED APPLES WITH A SEA GREENS & RUM CARAMEL SAUCE

Seaweed isn't the first thing that springs to mind when you think of baked apples, but in much the same way that salt enhances the flavour of sweet things, the smoky flavour of the dulse complements the creamy caramel sauce, bringing out the buttery notes and providing the perfect counterfoil to the tart apples.

Serves 4

75g/3oz/6 tbsp butter
75g/3oz/6 tbsp caster (superfine) sugar
75g/3oz/¾ cup ground almonds
100g/3¾oz/⅔ cup sultanas (golden raisins)
50g/2oz fresh dulse, chopped, or 10g/¼oz flaked dulse
5ml/1 tsp ground cinnamon
4 cooking apples

For the caramel sauce

300g/11oz/1½ cups white caster (superfine) sugar
about 75ml/5 tbsp water
a drop of lemon juice
75g/3oz/6 tbsp butter
175ml/6fl oz/¾ cup double (heavy) cream or coconut cream
10g/¹⁄₂₄oz flaked sea greens
30ml/2 tbsp dark rum

Preheat the oven to 160°C/325°F/Gas 3. Cream the butter and sugar together in a bowl with a wooden spoon. Add the ground almonds, sultanas, dulse and cinnamon and mix to combine.

Core the apples, place them in a roasting pan and stuff them with the sultana mixture, making sure it goes down the cavity. Bake for 45 minutes, until soft.

Meanwhile, make the sauce. Put the sugar in a deep, heavy pan and add just enough water to dampen the sugar all over. Over a medium heat, dissolve the sugar in the water, without boiling it, until every grain of sugar has dissolved. Do not stir.

Once the sugar syrup has formed, add the lemon juice and bring it to the boil. Boil steadily, without stirring, for about 5 minutes, until the liquid is amber in colour. You may need to swirl the pan a few times. Stay with the pan and take great care. Remove the pan from the heat and let it cool slightly.

Stir in the butter and cream. This will cause the caramel to bubble, so wear oven mitts and take care. Stir in the flaked sea greens and rum and set aside until the apples are baked.

Pour the sauce over the baked apples, or serve them separately, putting the sauce in a jug or pitcher.

Cook's tip
Making caramel is quite tricky, so follow the instructions carefully and don't try to rush it. Stirring will cause the sugar to crystallise, which ruins the caramel, so swirling only is recommended. Since hot sugar gives very nasty burns, it is extremely important to take great care and wear oven mitts when you add the flaked sea greens and cream. This is a really sweet dessert so for a slightly less sweet version add half the quantity of sugar to the sauce and apples.

BLACKBERRY, APPLE & DULSE CRUMBLE

This classic family favourite is a forager's delight: pick the blackberries in the hedgerows, scrump some windfalls (with permission) and get down to the sea shore to find some fresh dulse. If this isn't possible, all of the ingredients can be bought instead, and you can use dried.

To make the filling, snip the dulse into small pieces with scissors and core and chop the apples.

Put the blackberries, apples, cinnamon, sugar, water and dulse into a large pan and simmer over a medium heat for about 15 minutes, until soft. Check frequently that it isn't drying out, and add a splash more water if necessary.

Remove from the heat, taste the mixture and add more sugar if necessary. Spoon into an ovenproof dish and set aside. Preheat the oven to 190°C/375°F/Gas 5.

To make the crumble, mix together the cinnamon and flour in a large bowl, then rub in the butter, until the mixture resembles breadcrumbs.

Stir in the sugar and oats, then spoon the crumble over the filling, patting it down slightly with the back of the spoon.

Place the dish on a baking sheet to catch any drips, and bake in the oven for about 30 minutes, until bubbling and golden.

Serve with a generous dollop of vanilla ice cream or a good slurp of cream and enjoy!

Serves 6

For the filling

25g/1oz fresh dulse or 5g/1oz dried dulse, chopped

3 eating apples

2 cooking apples

200g/7oz blackberries

10ml/2 tsp ground cinnamon

30ml/2 tbsp demerara (raw) sugar

15ml/1 tbsp water

For the crumble

5ml/1 tsp ground cinnamon

115g/4oz/1 cup plain (all-purpose) flour

75g/3oz/6 tbsp butter, cubed

25g/1oz/2 tbsp demerara (raw) sugar

60ml/4 tbsp rolled oats

vanilla ice cream or cream, to serve

DAIRY-FREE CHOCOLATE MOUSSE

Using avocados and coconut cream in place of the usual chocolate and cream not only makes this thick, intense mousse dairy-free, but it also increases its health benefits too. Mood-enhancing cacao has one of the highest levels of antioxidants of all foods, while the ground sea greens further boost the beneficial properties of this delicious dessert.

Serves 2–4

1–2 frozen ripe bananas
1–2 chilled avocados
45ml/3 tbsp cacao powder or unsweetened cocoa powder
about 30ml/2 tbsp honey
5ml/1 tsp lemon juice
5ml/1 tsp vanilla extract
90ml/6 tbsp coconut cream
5ml/1 tsp ground sea greens
fresh berries, to serve (optional)

Peel 1 banana, then weigh the flesh. Cut 1 avocado in half, remove the stone, then scoop the flesh into a bowl and weigh that, too. Add more banana or avocado as required until you have an equal weight of each. Roughly chop the banana.

Put the banana and avocado flesh in a food processor or blender and add all the remaining ingredients.

Blitz until a smooth paste forms, stopping and scraping down the sides as required.

Taste, and add a little more honey if you prefer the mousse sweeter, and a little more coconut cream if it is too thick (or if you want larger portions!).

Divide the mousse between two to four ramekins, small glasses or small dishes, depending on their size, and serve immediately. Alternatively, chill in the refrigerator until required. It is best eaten at room temperature, so remove it from the refrigerator 30 minutes before you intend to eat it.

CARRAGEEN VANILLA JELLY

Irish moss, or carrageen, has traditionally been employed as a setting agent for centuries, used to make a wide range of jellies and blancmanges. Ideal for those who prefer not to use gelatine, it has no flavour but does bring nutritional benefits to the table, meaning you can enjoy this low-sugar milk jelly (almost) guilt-free.

Serves 4

10g/¼oz dried carrageen

750ml/1¼ pints/3 cups nut, oat, soya or dairy milk

1 egg yolk

30ml/2 tbsp sugar or a refined-sugar replacement, such as Stevia or honey

a few drops of vanilla extract

summer berries, compote or fresh, to serve

Place the carrageen in the pan with the milk, bring to the boil and simmer for 15–20 minutes. During this time the carrageen will become gelatinous and break up, thickening the mixture enough to coat a spoon. If the mixture reduces too much add a little more milk as you go.

Strain the thickened milk into a bowl, then return the mixture to the pan, whisking in the egg yolk, sugar or its replacement, and vanilla extract.

Simmer for 2–3 minutes to cook the egg, stirring constantly to prevent it from catching on the base of the pan.

Pour the mixture into ramekins or glasses and leave to set for 3–4 hours. Serve topped with compote or fresh currants or berries.

CHAI SEAWEED PANNA COTTA WITH MANGO

This fusion dish combines the Indian flavours of chai and mango with an Italian classic, panna cotta, which means 'cooked cream'. Some of the cream has been replaced with yogurt to lighten this version, adding a sourness that perfectly complements the warm spices. Traditionally made with gelatine, here dried carrageen has been employed instead as a setting agent.

First make the panna cotta. Put the milk, spices and carrageen in a pan and simmer gently for 7–10 minutes, until the milk has thickened slightly. Add the teabag and allow it to brew for a couple of minutes – don't let it brew for too long!

Remove the teabag and push the mixture through a fine strainer into a bowl. Set aside.

Put the yogurt, cream and sugar in a pan and bring it gently to the boil. Remove from the heat as soon as it boils and stir the mixture into the infused milk.

Grease six moulds or ramekins and place a disc of baking parchment in the bottom. Evenly divide the panna cotta mixture between the moulds and leave to cool. Transfer to the refrigerator for 6 hours to set.

To release the panna cotta, dip the bases and sides of the moulds or ramekins very briefly in a bowl of hot water (take care not to get the surface of the panna cotta wet), and upturn them on to dessert plates. Place the plates in the refrigerator while you prepare the mango.

To make the mango accompaniment, preheat a heavy griddle over a medium heat.

Melt the coconut oil in the microwave for a few seconds, then use it to brush the mango slices. Sprinkle some sugar on one side of the slices, then place them sugar-side down on the griddle and chargrill for about 1 minute, or until black lines appear on the fruit.

Sprinkle the tops of the slices with sugar and flip them over, then chargrill for a further minute. Pour over the rum (if using) and allow to cook for a few seconds.

Serve immediately with the cold panna cotta.

Serves 6

For the panna cotta

500ml/17fl oz/generous 2 cups full-fat (whole) milk

1 cinnamon stick

2 cloves

2 cardamom pods, crushed

a pinch of grated nutmeg

3g/¹⁄₁₂oz dried carrageen

1 chai teabag

200ml/7fl oz/scant 1 cup natural Greek (US strained plain) yogurt

500ml/17fl oz/generous 2 cups double (heavy) cream

115g/4oz/1 cup soft light brown sugar

butter or oil, for greasing the moulds

For the mango

5ml/1 tsp coconut oil

1 mango (not too ripe!), peeled, pitted and sliced into 12 even-size wedges

5ml/1 tsp soft light brown sugar

a splash of rum (optional)

Cook's tip

Carrageen is actually a red seaweed but it can be dried in such a way that it bleaches in the sun. This makes it more aesthetically pleasing for creamy desserts such as this, and several others in this chapter. Fresh carrageen could be used instead but we'd recommend soaking it for at least an hour to remove all traces of saltiness.

TANGY RASPBERRY MOSS POTS

This soft, white, creamy dessert is a dream to eat and the perfect foil to the summer's finest berries, although you could use many other types of fruit instead, such as blueberries, sliced pear, apple compote, sliced mango… the list goes on. Be careful when measuring out the carrageen, since using too much makes the texture very gelatinous and unpleasant.

Serves 4–6

8g/⅕oz dried carrageen

400ml/14fl oz/1⅔ cups water

60ml/4 tbsp sugar

2 eggs, separated

2 lemons

150g/5oz raspberries

Break the carrageen into small pieces and put it in a pan with the water. Simmer gently for 15 minutes, stirring frequently. Remove the pan from the heat and leave to cool slightly for 2–3 minutes.

Place the sugar and egg yolks in a bowl and whisk together.

Put the egg whites in a separate bowl and whisk until stiff peaks form.

Roll the lemons on a hard surface to help release their juice, then grate them, slice them in half and squeeze the juice.

Pour the carrageen gel through a strainer into another large bowl and push it through with the back of a spoon.

Stir in most of the lemon rind (reserve some for a garnish) and juice and mix well, then whisk in the egg yolks. Carefully fold in the egg whites using a metal spoon, until all the lumps have disappeared, trying not to knock out too much air.

Put a few of the raspberries in the bottom of each of four small glasses or six ramekins then spoon over a layer of the carrageen mixture. Add a few more raspberries (reserving some for the top), then spoon over all of the remaining carrageen mixture.

Allow the pots to cool, then place them in the refrigerator for a minimum of 30 minutes or until they have set.

Decorate the tops with the reserved raspberries and lemon zest and serve.

RAW CHEESECAKE

This refined-sugar free dessert takes a little time to make, but each stage is very simple and the results more than reward the effort. It is suitable for vegans and ideal as a make-ahead showstopper for a dinner party or special meal, and tastes all the better for the fact that it's packed with goodness and far less fat and sugar than standard cheesecakes. Seaweed plays a starring role in two of the three components, lending seasoning and flavour to the base and acting as a setting agent for the creamy cashew-nut filling.

Serves 8–10

For the base

300g/11oz/1½ cups chopped walnuts or almonds

30ml/2 tbsp flaked sea salad

150g/5oz/1 cup fresh dates (such as Medjool)

For the filling

200g/7oz/scant 2 cups unsalted cashew nuts

20g/¾ oz dried carrageen

300ml/½ pint/1¼ cups water

22.5ml/1½ tbsp agave nectar

5ml/1 tsp vanilla extract

juice and grated rind of 2 lemons

50g/2oz/¼ cup cocoa butter

up to 150ml/¼ pint/⅔ cup water

For the topping

225g/8oz/2 cups frozen berries of choice

10ml/2 tsp agave nectar

15ml/1 tbsp psyllium husk powder

Cook's tip

Psyllium husk powder is a thickener that has the added benefit of being high in soluble fibre. It forms a gel when it comes into contact with moisture, giving the berry topping a slightly gelatinous texture that means it doesn't just flow off the top of the cheesecake. It can be bought from health-food stores and some supermarkets.

Put the walnuts or almonds for the base and the cashew nuts for the filling in separate bowls of cold water and leave to soak for at least 4 hours, but preferably overnight.

For the filling, snip the carrageen into small pieces and put it in a bowl with the water. Leave it to soak overnight, then pour the whole lot into a food processor and whizz until becomes gel-like. Transfer to a bowl and rinse out the food processor.

For the base, drain the almonds or walnuts then put them in the food processor with the flaked sea salad and blend until the nuts are finely chopped. Add the dates and blend again until a fairly sticky mixture forms that binds together.

Press the date-and-nut mixture into the bottom of a 23cm/9in loose-based flan tin or pan using the back of a spoon, and leave it to chill in the refrigerator while you finish making the filling.

Put the agave nectar, vanilla extract, lemon juice and rind, cocoa butter, and carrageen gel in a blender and process until it is smooth.

Drain the cashew nuts, then add them to the carrageen mixture and blend again. You may need to add some water at this stage to enable blending, but it should not be runny.

Pour the filling over the chilled base and smooth over the top, then put it in the freezer for 30 minutes while you make the fruity topping.

For the topping, blend the berries, agave nectar and psyllium husk powder in a blender until smooth, then spread it evenly over the top of the base. Return the cheesecake to the freezer to set. Alternatively, you could serve the topping as an accompaniment and spoon it over the set cheesecake when serving it.

CHOCOLATE TART WITH DULSE CARAMEL

This stunning chocolate tart is as nutritious as it is attractive, packed with antioxidants from the chocolate and the cocoa and benefiting from the myriad vitamins and minerals supplied by the sea salad used in the tart's base and the dulse in the unusual caramelised topping. Not your everyday tart!

Serves 6–8

For the base

15ml/1 tbsp flaked sea salad

190g/6½oz/1⅔ cups plain (all-purpose) flour

30ml/2 tbsp caster (superfine) sugar

125g/4¼oz/generous ½ cup cold butter, diced

1 egg yolk

about 30ml/2 tbsp water

50g/2oz/½ cup blanched hazelnuts, finely chopped

For the filling

100g/3¾oz dark (bittersweet) chocolate (minimum 70 per cent cocoa solids)

75g/3oz/6 tbsp butter

2 eggs, plus the remaining egg white from the pastry

45ml/3 tbsp caster (superfine) sugar

15ml/1 tbsp unsweetened cocoa powder

For the dulse caramel

30ml/2 tbsp flaked dulse or 75g/3oz fresh dulse, chopped into very small pieces

75g/3oz/generous ¼ cup caster (superfine) sugar

25g/1oz/2 tbsp butter

100ml/3½fl oz/scant ½ cup double (heavy) cream

For the base, put the sea salad, flour and sugar in a large bowl and stir to combine well. Rub in the cold butter, until the mixture resembles breadcrumbs and starts to come together, then add the egg yolk and up to 30ml/2 tbsp water and mix again, until a pastry dough forms.

Shape the pastry into a ball, wrap it in clear film or plastic wrap and chill it in the refrigerator for at least 30 minutes.

Roll out the pastry dough on a lightly floured surface until it is thin and large enough to fill the base and sides of a 20cm/8in loose-based tart tin or pan. Carefully lift and fit the pastry in the tin or pan, pressing down in the corners so it fits well. Do not trim off the edges where they overhang.

Put the pastry in the refrigerator while you preheat the oven to 180°C/350°F/Gas 4. Place a baking sheet in the oven.

Once the oven is up to temperature, cover the pastry with baking parchment and fill it with baking beans. Place the tin or pan on the hot baking sheet and blind-bake the pastry for about 20 minutes, then remove the paper and baking beans and bake for a further 10 minutes, until golden.

Remove from the oven and leave to cool for a few minutes, then carefully trim away the overhanging pastry with a serrated knife. Set aside and leave to cool.

...continued overleaf

For the filling, put the chocolate and butter in a heatproof bowl and position this over a pan of barely simmering water. Leave to melt, stirring briefly to combine.

Meanwhile, whisk the eggs and sugar in a bowl using an electric mixer for about 5 minutes, until the mixture thickens and increases greatly in volume.

Stir a spoonful of the egg mixture into the chocolate mixture to loosen it, then carefully fold in the remaining egg mixture. Sift over the cocoa powder and very gently stir to combine fully, without knocking out all of the air.

Sprinkle the hazelnuts over the cooled tart base, then pour in the chocolate mixture. Return the tart to the still-hot oven and bake for 25 minutes, until set.

Meanwhile, make the dulse caramel. Soak the flaked dulse in 30ml/2 tbsp hot water for 5 minutes, then drain and set aside. This is not necessary if you are using fresh dulse.

Put the sugar in a deep, heavy pan and add just enough water to dampen the sugar all over. Over a medium heat, dissolve the sugar in the water, without boiling it, until every grain of sugar has dissolved. Do not stir.

Once the sugar syrup has formed, bring it to the boil. Boil steadily, without stirring, for about 5 minutes, until the liquid is amber in colour. You may need to swirl the pan a few times. Stay with the pan and take great care. If sugar crystals start to form around the edge of the pan, use a heatproof pastry brush dipped in water to very carefully brush them back into the syrup, letting the water carry them downwards.

Remove the pan from the heat and let the caramel cool slightly, then add the soaked flaked dulse or finely chopped fresh dulse, butter and cream. This will cause the caramel to bubble, so wear oven gloves and take care.

Remove the baked tart from the oven and leave to cool, then serve with the dulse caramel.

PEPPER TRUFFLES

The ultimate way to round off a meal, truffles are really simple to make and keep extremely well in the freezer, if you don't scoff the lot in one sitting. You could also of course halve the quantities and make fewer truffles. It's fairly common to season chocolate these days, and the pepper dulse in these really brings out the intense cacao flavour. For the most striking effect, divide the rolled truffles into two. Coat one batch with unsweetened cocoa powder, and dip the other in melted chocolate and then roll the balls in chopped nuts.

Finely chop 300g/11oz of the chocolate and place it in a large heatproof bowl.

Put the cream and butter into a pan and heat gently until the butter melts and the cream just reaches simmering point.

Remove the cream mixture from the heat and pour it over the broken chocolate pieces. Stir to create a smooth mixture. Stir in the pepper dulse and leave the mixture to cool at room temperature for 4 hours.

Line a large baking sheet with baking parchment and lightly dab your hands with the oil. Put the chopped nuts in one bowl and the cocoa powder in another.

Take a teaspoon of the mixture and roll it between your palms to shape the truffle, or shape it with two spoons. Roll the first 20 or so in cocoa powder as soon as you have shaped each one, then place them on the paper.

Shape the remainder of the mixture into balls but don't coat them in cocoa powder. Instead, place them in the refrigerator to firm up while you melt the remaining 100g/3oz chocolate in a heatproof bowl over a pan of barely simmering water.

Makes about 40

400g/14oz good-quality dark (bittersweet) chocolate (minimum 70 per cent cocoa solids)
300ml/½ pint/1¼ cups double (heavy) cream
50g/2oz/¼ cup unsalted butter
15ml/1 tbsp ground pepper dulse
sunflower or rapeseed oil, for greasing hands
45–60ml/3–4 tbsp chopped nuts, for coating
30–45ml/2–3 tbsp unsweetened cocoa powder, for coating

Once melted, allow the chocolate to cool slightly so it thickens and doesn't run straight off the truffles.

With a fork, pick up one uncoated truffle at a time and hold it over the bowl of melted chocolate. Spoon the chocolate over the truffle until it is well coated, then roll it in the chopped nuts and return it to the paper on the baking sheet. Repeat with the remaining truffles.

Leave all the truffles to firm up for a few hours, then transfer them to an airtight container and store them in the refrigerator for up to a week, or in the freezer for up to a month. To defrost, simply remove however many truffles you want and place them on a plate at room temperature for about 20 minutes.

Chapter 6
BAKING

Baking seaweed brings out an earthy depth of flavour that is both incredibly tasty and comforting without being overpowering, which is probably one of the reasons why it has been used in this way for centuries.

From bread and pastries to cakes and cookies, this collection of recipes shows how seaweed can really transform both sweet and savoury baked treats. Some, such as oatcakes or breads, are wholesome and nutritious – perfect for providing nourishment on a daily basis, while others are a little more indulgent.

One example of the latter is the ever-popular chocolate brownies, in which the salty flavour of the dulse lifts the sweet richness of the chocolate to create absolute harmony. Or for a more seaweedy hit you could try out the seeded carrot cake with its sea spaghetti twist and distinctive sea-green garnish. Enjoy!

RHUBARB, DATE & NORI SLICES

This recipe is an adapted version of date slices made by a lovely woman called Binky, who has been one of our seaweed packers for many years now. The nori gives the dish a nutty additional taste and the rhubarb provides a delicious tartness.

Preheat the oven to 180°C/350°F/Gas 4. Grease a 25cm/10in baking tin or pan with butter.

To make the filling, put the rhubarb and dates into a pan. Add the orange juice and cinnamon and simmer gently over a low heat, stirring occasionally, for about 10 minutes, until softened and jam-like in consistency. Set aside to cool.

Meanwhile, make the topping/base. Put the oats, sugar, flour and nori in a large bowl and mix to combine well, then blend in the butter.

Beat the eggs in a separate bowl, then add them to the topping/base mixture and stir to combine.

Press about half of the oat mixture evenly into the bottom of the greased tin. Spoon the fruit mixture on top and spread it evenly, then dot and press the remainder of the oat mixture on top.

Bake for about 45 minutes, until it is golden brown and smelling heavenly.

Leave to cool in the tin before carefully turning out and cutting into squares or rectangles.

Makes 16 pieces

For the filling

4 rhubarb stalks, chopped into small pieces

250g/9oz/1½ cups chopped dried stoned (pitted) dates

100ml/3½fl oz/scant ½ cup orange juice

2.5ml/½ tsp ground cinnamon

For the topping/base

150g/5oz/10 tbsp slightly salted butter, softened, plus extra for greasing the tin or pan

200g/7oz/generous 2 cups rolled oats

200g/7oz/1 cup demerara (raw) sugar

50g/2oz/½ cup plain (all-purpose) flour

10g/¼oz flaked nori

2 eggs

Cook's tip

If nori is unavailable then sea salad or dulse flakes can be used in the same way instead.

CHILLI, WALNUT & ORANGE GLUTEN-FREE CHOCOLATE BROWNIES

Chilli, orange, nuts and salt are classic flavourings for chocolate, and in these scrumptious gluten-free brownies they all appear at once, with an extra flavour dimension in the form of some sea greens or dulse. As well as being an indulgent teatime treat, these make a fantastic dessert served with a dollop of crème fraîche mixed with some orange zest.

Makes about 16

200g/7oz good-quality dark (bittersweet) chocolate (minimum 70 per cent cocoa solids)
250g/9oz/generous 1 cup unsalted butter
5ml/1 tsp coconut oil or olive oil
3g/¹⁄₁₂oz dried sea greens or 5g/¹⁄₈oz dried dulse, finely chopped
a pinch of seaweed salt
50g/2oz/½ cup chopped walnuts
5ml/1 tsp chilli flakes
juice and rind of 1 large orange
75g/3oz/²⁄₃ cup unsweetened cocoa powder, plus extra for dusting
65g/2½oz/9 tbsp finely ground almonds or almond flour
5ml/1 tsp baking powder
250g/9oz/generous 1 cup soft dark brown sugar
4 large (US extra large) eggs

Preheat the oven to 180°C/350°F/Gas 4. Line a 25cm/10in square baking tin or pan with baking parchment.

Put the chocolate and butter in a large heatproof bowl over a pan of barely simmering water and heat until melted, stirring once or twice to combine, until smooth. Remove from the heat and set aside.

Heat the oil in a frying pan and add the dried sea greens, if using. Fry over a medium heat for 2–3 minutes, until the sea greens are crispy. Add to the chocolate along with the seaweed salt. If using chopped dulse, just add it to the chocolate mixture as it is, without first frying it.

Add the walnuts, chilli flakes and orange juice to the chocolate mixture and stir together well.

In a separate bowl, mix together the cocoa powder, ground almonds or almond flour, baking powder and soft dark brown sugar. Add this to the chocolate mixture and stir together well.

...continued overleaf

Beat the eggs in a separate bowl, then add them to the brownie mixture and stir until you achieve a silky consistency.

Pour the mixture into the prepared tin and bake for about 25 minutes. Start checking the brownies after about 20 minutes – you don't want to overcook them so, unlike cakes, you don't want a skewer inserted into the middle of the brownie to come out all clean; the brownies should be slightly springy on the outside but still gooey in the middle.

Remove from the oven and allow to cool in the tin, then turn out, dust with sifted cocoa powder, and cut into chunky squares.

Variation

If you aren't so keen on spicy sweet food, or can't abide chocolate orange, do feel free to omit these additional flavourings, although we promise they do work exceedingly well together.

CARROT, SEA SPAGHETTI & PUMPKIN SEED CAKE

This perfectly moist and delicious cake is an all-time classic given a seaweedy twist with the addition of a little sea spaghetti in the cake mixture and, an optional extra for the true seaweed lover, some vivid sea greens layered with the icing.

Serves 6–8

2 oranges

10g/¼oz dried sea spaghetti or 65g/2½oz fresh sea spaghetti, chopped into 1cm/½in pieces

100g/3¾oz/⅔ cup pumpkin seeds

150ml/¼ pint/⅔ cup sunflower oil

200g/7oz/1 cup soft light brown sugar

4 large (US extra large) eggs

225g/8oz/2 cups self-raising (self-rising) flour

5ml/1 tsp ground cinnamon

5ml/1 tsp ground ginger

2.5ml/½ tsp grated nutmeg

5ml/1 tsp bicarbonate of soda (baking soda)

175g/6oz/generous 1 cup grated carrots

100g/3¾oz/⅔ cup sultanas (golden raisins)

For the icing

250g/9oz/generous 1 cup full-fat cream cheese

75g/3oz/⅔ cup icing (confectioners') sugar

grated rind and juice of 1 orange

optional extras: chopped nuts, chopped crystallized ginger, vanilla extract, ground cinnamon, finely grated carrot, finely chopped rehydrated sea greens

Preheat the oven to 180°C/350°F/Gas 4. Grease an 18cm/7in square baking tin or pan and line it with baking parchment.

Grate the rind from the oranges and set aside. Squeeze the juice into a bowl, then add the dried sea spaghetti and set aside to rehydrate for about 10 minutes. You can omit this step if you are using fresh sea spaghetti.

Heat a small frying pan over a medium heat, then add the pumpkin seeds and toast them for about 2 minutes, shaking them occasionally and staying with them so they don't burn.

Put the oil, sugar and eggs in a large bowl and whisk together until well combined.

Mix together the flour, cinnamon, ginger, nutmeg and bicarbonate of soda, then sift this into the wet mixture, stirring as you go, until just combined.

Finally, add the toasted seeds, grated carrots, sultanas, sea spaghetti and orange juice and stir well. The cake mixture should be fairly runny.

Pour the mixture into the baking tin and bake for about 45 minutes. You can test the cake by inserting a skewer; if it comes out clean then it's cooked. Remove from the oven and leave it in the tin for a few minutes before turning out on to a cooling rack.

Mix together all the icing ingredients. If you plan to eat the cake immediately, spread the cream cheese icing all over the completely cool cake, or cut it in half and sandwich it together with icing and perhaps some sea greens before covering the outside with more icing and topping with chopped nuts, as shown in the photograph. If you intend to keep the cake for a few days, store the cake and the icing separately in airtight containers in the refrigerator, then slice and slather with icing as required.

SEA BAKLAVA

This is a tasty seaweed twist on a Mediterranean classic; the slight saltiness of the sea greens enhances the sweetness of the honey in much the same way that salt boosts caramel.

Makes about 15 pieces

For the baklava

300g/11oz/1½ cups unsalted mixed nuts
5ml/1 tsp ground sea greens
10ml/2 tsp ground cinnamon
a pinch of ground cloves
200g/7oz/scant 1 cup unsalted butter, melted
12 sheets of filo pastry

For the syrup

300g/11oz/1½ cups white sugar
300ml/½ pint/1¼ cups water
100ml/3½fl oz/scant ½ cup clear honey
5ml/1 tsp ground sea greens
peeled rind of 1 orange, pith scraped off
1 cinnamon stick

Preheat the oven to 180°C/350°F/Gas 4.

First, make the syrup by placing all the ingredients in a medium pan and simmering over a medium heat for about 15 minutes, until thick and glossy. Remove the cinnamon and orange rind and leave to cool. (The syrup must be cool when you pour it over the baklava, to stop it from becoming soggy.)

Meanwhile, make the baklava. Grind the nuts, sea greens and spices together in a food processor or with a mortar and pestle until they have the consistency of home-made breadcrumbs.

Lightly grease a shallow tin or pan with a little of the melted butter (line it with baking parchment if it doesn't have a non-stick coating).

Working with one sheet at a time and keeping the remainder covered with a damp dish towel to prevent it from cracking, lay a sheet of filo on a lightly floured surface and brush it all over with melted butter. Place the buttered pastry in the tin and butter another three sheets of filo, placing them on top of each other.

When you have layered four sheets of filo, sprinkle one-third of the nut mixture over the top, spreading it in an even layer. Repeat twice more, then cover the top layer of nuts with a final four sheets of filo and brush with butter. Score the top few layers of pastry with a sharp knife into a diamond pattern.

Bake in the middle of the preheated oven for 15 minutes, or until golden on top. Keep a close eye on it in the final few minutes, as the pastry can quickly burn. Remove from the oven and spoon half of the syrup over the top. Leave this to sink in for 5 minutes, then spoon over the rest.

Leave the baklava to cool before turning it out and cutting it along the scored lines into diamond-shaped pieces.

SEA SPAGHETTI & NUT BANANA BREAD

This bread is a great way to use up old bananas and make a not-too-sweet cake/bread.
The nuts bring crunch and the seaweed brings a chewy texture to a simple recipe,
along with the goodness contained by both ingredients.

Makes 1 loaf

3 very ripe bananas

75g/3oz/⅓ cup butter, melted

5ml/1 tsp bicarbonate of soda (baking soda)

a pinch of salt

90g/3½oz/½ cup soft light brown sugar

1 egg, beaten

5ml/1 tsp vanilla extract

175g/6oz/1½ cups plain (all-purpose) flour

25g/1oz fresh sea spaghetti or 10g/¼oz dried sea spaghetti, rehydrated in cold water for 10 minutes, chopped into 5mm/¼in pieces

Preheat the oven to 180°C/350°F/Gas 4. Grease a 20 x 10cm/ 8 x 4in loaf tin or pan and line it with baking parchment.

Put the bananas in a large bowl, mash them with a fork, then stir in the melted butter.

Add the bicarbonate of soda, salt, brown sugar, beaten egg and vanilla extract, then stir in the flour and mix well to just combine. Stir in the sea spaghetti.

Pour the mixture into the loaf tin and cook for 50–60 minutes, until a skewer inserted into the middle comes out clean. If there is any sticky mixture on the skewer, bake the bread for a further 5–10 minutes.

Remove from the oven and leave to cool slightly in the tin for 10 minutes, then turn out the bread on to a wire rack to cool completely.

Cook's tip
This freezes well, so if you don't want to eat it all, cut off the section you want to keep for another day, slice it and stash in the freezer. To defrost it, simply put it on a plate and leave it at room temperature for about 15 minutes.

CHEESE & DULSE SCONES

Savoury scones are perfect picnic fare, being portable and delicious on their own, although they are even more scrummy warm and spread with butter. They are also a fantastic alternative to dumplings to serve with stew. Dulse and cheese works as well as the more common yeast extract and cheese combination, and gives the scones a pleasingly speckled finish. As with making pastry, it is important to handle the mix as little as possible; grating the butter means that less rubbing and manhandling is required.

Preheat the oven to 220°C/425°F/Gas 7. Liberally dust a couple of baking sheets with some flour.

Mix together all the dry ingredients in a large bowl, then add the grated butter and cheese. Using your fingertips, rub in the fat until the mixture has the consistency of breadcrumbs.

Gradually add the milk, mixing well until you have a fairly slack but not-too-wet dough. You may not need all the milk.

...continued overleaf

Makes about 8–10 large or 15–20 smaller scones

450g/1lb/4 cups self-raising (self-rising) flour, plus extra for dusting

5ml/1 tsp mustard powder

a pinch of cayenne pepper

a pinch of ground black pepper

2.5ml/½ tsp bicarbonate of soda (baking soda)

3g/1/2oz flaked dulse or 15g/½oz fresh dulse, snipped into little pieces

50g/2oz/¼ cup cold butter, grated

50g/2oz/½ cup grated strong Cheddar cheese, plus extra for sprinkling

about 225ml/7½fl oz/scant 1 cup milk, plus extra for brushing

Turn out the dough on to a well-floured surface and use your hands to fold the dough in half. Turn it through 90 degrees and fold it in half again, to ensure all the flour is incorporated without working the dough too much.

Roll or pat out the dough to a thickness of about 2.5cm/1in. Decide whether you want to make large (9cm/3¾in) or small (5cm/2in) scones, then dip the chosen cutter in flour and stamp out as many rounds as you can. Do not twist the dough, just press straight down and lift up again.

Transfer the rounds to the prepared baking sheets, then gather together the remaining dough and re-roll it, then stamp again and repeat until all the dough is used. Try not to work it too much as you re-roll it.

Brush the tops with milk and sprinkle with a little extra cheese and bake for 10–15 minutes (depending on their size), until risen and golden and the cheese has melted.

Remove the scones from the oven and transfer to a wire rack. Serve warm or cold. Store any leftovers in an airtight container for 2–3 days and, for best results, refresh in a hot oven for 5 minutes before eating.

SEA SALAD OAT CAKES

These speckled oat cakes are a healthy snack since the oats release their energy slowly, keeping you fuller for longer and helping to maintain steady blood-sugar levels. Sea salad is the dominant flavouring, making them savoury and moreish – the perfect partner for cheese and chutney, or even some seaweed pesto if you want a really good seaweed hit.

Preheat the oven to 180°C/350°F/Gas 4 and line two baking sheets with baking parchment.

Mix together all the ingredients apart from the oil and water in a bowl. Form a well in the middle and pour in the oil and then enough boiling water to form a firm, but not sticky, dough. If it's too sticky, add more oatmeal.

Form the oatcake dough into a ball and leave it to rest for 5-10 minutes, so that the oats and oatmeal can absorb the liquid, swell and stick together.

Turn out the dough on to a lightly floured surface and roll it out to a thickness of about 5mm/¼in.

Using a 6cm/2½in cookie cutter, stamp out rounds and transfer them to the prepared baking sheets. Gather together the remaining dough, re-roll it and stamp out more rounds until all of the dough is used.

Bake for 20 minutes, then turn and bake for a further 5-10 minutes, until firm and dry all over. Remove them from the oven and transfer to a wire rack to cool completely.

Store in an airtight container for up to 2 weeks.

Makes 15–20

225g/8oz/2 cups oatmeal

200g/7oz/2 cups rolled oats

75g/3oz/1 cup fresh sea salad or dulse, or 15g/½oz dried sea salad or dulse, rehydrated in cold water for 20 minutes, finely chopped

10 twists of black pepper or ground pepper dulse

2.5ml/½ tsp salt

a handful of sesame seeds (optional)

75ml/5 tbsp extra virgin olive oil

boiling water

SEA GREENS SODA BREAD

Soda bread is a delicious, slightly cakey alternative to leavened (yeast-risen) bread. Quick to make, it works wonderfully well with the addition of seaweed. This recipe uses sea greens, which gives it a fresh sorrel-like flavour, but you could try experimenting with pepper dulse or dulse for a smoky spiciness. The trick to good soda bread is to mix the dough quickly for a light fluffy loaf and to make sure the oven is really hot before you start.

Preheat the oven to 190°C/375°F/Gas 5. Line a heavy baking sheet with baking parchment.

Sift together the flours, bicarbonate of soda, salt and sugar (if using) into a large bowl, then stir in the sea greens.

Make a well in the middle and pour in the buttermilk. Mix with your hands or a spoon to form a soft dough – this should be slack but not too wet.

Sprinkle some flour on your hands and a work surface, then tip out the bread on to the surface and knead it briefly until it's smooth.

Sprinkle the surface with flour, then lightly roll it out into a round, shaping it with your hands. Using a large, sharp knife, slash a cross into the top of the loaf. This allows the loaf to cook evenly. Transfer the loaf to the baking sheet.

Bake for 35–40 minutes, until risen and golden. When it's cooked, the loaf should sound hollow when you tap the bottom and feel light and fluffy when you pick it up.

Remove the bread from the oven and transfer it to a wire rack to cool.

Cook's tip

Buttermilk is basically sour milk and can be bought in many supermarkets. You can create a substitute at home by mixing together 300ml/½ pint/1¼ cups full-fat (whole) milk and a good squeeze of lemon juice, then leaving it to stand for 15–20 minutes at room temperature until it starts to curdle (include the curdled bits in the recipe).

Makes 1 loaf

250g/9oz/generous 1 cup wholemeal (whole-wheat) flour, plus extra for dusting
200g/6½oz/1⅔ cups strong white bread flour
5ml/1 tsp bicarbonate of soda (baking soda)
5ml/1 tsp salt
5ml/1 tsp soft light brown sugar (optional)
10g/¼oz flaked sea greens
300ml/½ pint/1¼ cups buttermilk (see Cook's tip)

GLUTEN-FREE DULSE FLATBREAD

Chickpea flour, or atta as it is known in India (and the name with which it may be labelled in Asian stores) is commonly used in Asia for making bread, and is nutritious as well as being gluten-free. These crispy flatbreads are extremely easy to make and taste so much better than any store-bought version, with the added bonus of being seasoned by flaked dulse, with all the benefits that brings.

Preheat the oven to 180°C/350°F/Gas 4. Line a baking sheet with baking parchment.

Rub together the flour and olive oil using your fingers, then stir in the dulse.

Pour in the water and stir until thoroughly mixed. The mixture will have a solid 'dough' consistency, but because there's no yeast, it does not need kneading.

Transfer the dough to a lightly floured work surface and shape it into six balls. This ensures that the pieces are about even in size.

Using a well-floured rolling pin, roll out each of the dough balls into circles about 5mm/¼in thick. Transfer to the prepared baking sheet.

Bake for 15–20 minutes, until the edges are slightly crispy, then remove from the oven and serve warm.

Cook's tip
These flatbreads can also be used as bases for pizzas. Simply prepare and bake as above, then add your chosen toppings, such as tomato sauce, griddled aubergine (eggplant) and cheese, and bake again for a couple of minutes.

Makes 6

130g/4½oz/generous 1 cup chickpea flour, plus extra for dusting
5ml/1 tsp olive oil
5ml/1 tsp flaked dulse
235ml/7½fl oz/scant 1 cup water

SEA SALAD & PEPPER DULSE BREAD ROLLS

Soft white bread rolls freshly baked from the oven are just irresistible, and these ones are made even more special with the addition of not one but two types of seaweed. If you prefer, you could swap half the white bread flour for some wholemeal bread flour, but don't be tempted to use just wholemeal flour or the rolls will be really heavy in texture.

If using fresh yeast, make a starter by placing the yeast in a bowl with the sugar, 115g/4oz/1 cup of the flour and 100ml/3½fl oz/scant ½ cup of the water. Mix to form a paste, then lift this up with a spoon and pour the remaining water underneath so the paste is floating. Leave in a warm place for 15 minutes; the starter should start to prove away from the water.

Put the remaining flour and water, seaweeds, butter, salt and the starter and its water into a mixer fitted with a dough hook and mix on medium speed for about 10 minutes, until a smooth and elastic dough is formed.

If you are using easy-blend yeast, simply put all the ingredients apart from the beaten egg and water glaze into the processor and process as above. If you prefer to make the dough by hand, combine the ingredients in a large bowl, then transfer to a lightly floured surface and knead for about 10 minutes.

Transfer the dough to a large bowl, cover with clear film or plastic wrap and leave to prove in a warm place for about 1 hour or until it has doubled in size. Flour two baking sheets. Put the dough on to a floured work surface and gently knock back or punch down by kneading it for a minute.

Roll out the dough with a floured rolling pin to a thickness of 4cm/1½in. Use a floured cutter to stamp out rounds, then place them on the floured baking sheets. Re-roll the remaining dough and stamp out more rounds, until all the dough is used.

Brush the tops with the egg and water glaze, then sprinkle over the flaked dulse or seeds. Cover loosely with clean dish towels and leave to prove for 15 minutes. Preheat the oven to 200°C/400°F/Gas 6.

Bake the rolls for about 12 minutes (depending on their size), or until risen and golden. Remove from the oven and transfer to a wire rack to cool.

Makes about 12

15g/1oz fresh yeast or 5ml/2 tsp easy-blend (rapid-rise) dried yeast
15ml/1 tbsp sugar
450g/1lb/4 cups strong white bread four, plus extra for dusting
300ml/½ pint/1¼ cups lukewarm water
10g/¼oz flaked sea salad
15ml/1 tbsp flaked pepper dulse or 5ml/1 tsp dried dulse
25g/1oz/2 tbsp butter, melted
5ml/1 tsp salt
beaten egg and water, to glaze
15ml/1 tbsp flaked pepper dulse or poppy seeds, for sprinkling

FOCACCIA WITH FLAKED SEA GREENS & ROSEMARY

This moist dimpled bread studded with rosemary tastes and smells wonderful, and is very easy to make. The saline notes of the sea greens seasons the bread and works really well with the pungent rosemary, though you could swap it for dulse for a smokier flavour.

Makes 1 focaccia

15g/1oz fresh yeast or 5ml/2 tsp easy-blend (rapid-rise) dried yeast

15ml/1 tbsp sugar

450g/1lb/4 cups strong white bread flour

325ml/11fl oz/scant 1½ cups lukewarm water

10ml/2 tsp salt

10g/¼oz flaked sea greens

5ml/1 tsp olive oil, plus extra for greasing and drizzling

a handful of small rosemary sprigs

If using fresh yeast, make a starter by placing the yeast in a bowl with the sugar, 115g/4oz/1 cup of the flour and 100ml/3½fl oz/scant ½ cup of the water. Mix to form a paste, then lift this up with a spoon and pour the remaining water underneath so the paste is floating. Leave in a warm place for 15 minutes; the starter should start to prove away from the water.

Put the remaining flour and water, salt, sea greens, olive oil and the starter and its water into a mixer fitted with a dough hook and mix on medium speed for about 10 minutes, until a smooth and elastic dough is formed. If you are using easy-blend yeast, simply put all the ingredients apart from the rosemary into the processor and process as above.

Alternatively, combine everything apart from the rosemary in a large bowl, then turn out the dough on to a lightly oiled surface and knead it by hand for about 10 minutes, until smooth and elastic. The dough should be fairly wet and may stick to your hands initially. Oil your hands and keep kneading; the dough will become less sticky as you work it.

Oil a large baking sheet. Roll out the dough on an oiled surface to a thickness of about 2.5cm/1in.

Transfer the dough to the prepared sheet and drizzle over more olive oil. Push dimples into the surface of the dough using your fingertips, then put little sprigs of rosemary in each.

Cover the bread loosely with a clean dish towel and leave it to prove in a warm place for 20–30 minutes, until risen and doubled in size. Preheat the oven to 220°C/425°F/Gas 7.

Bake the focaccia in the oven for 10 minutes, then reduce the temperature to 180°C/350°F/Gas 4 and bake for a further 10 minutes, until risen and golden. Transfer to a wire rack to cool slightly – it is best enjoyed warm.

Chapter 7
DRINKS

Putting the recipes for this section together was, as you might imagine, pure pleasure. We don't like to go on about it, but seaweed is very, very good for you. However, does it then follow that adding seaweed to alcohol will make that good for you too? Well, we wouldn't like to go that far – all we can say is that it certainly tastes marvellous!

To balance out the adult-only treats, we've also added some incredibly healthy drinks suitable for all the family. Blending together lovely things takes next to no time, enabling you to get your seaweed hit in a hurry for a boost any time of day.

What's more, you can use these recipes as a basis for all sorts of juices, smoothies and boozy tipples – you'll soon find that adding seaweed to drinks to benefit from the intense nutrition and flavour becomes second nature.

BOOZY CHILLI & CARRAGEEN HOT CHOCOLATE

This intense, spicy, boozy drink is perfect for nights spent huddling around a fire, but is definitely one for grown-ups only! Carrageen makes this hot chocolate even thicker and more silky than usual, meaning it could almost be served as a dessert if you chill it and serve it with a spoon.

Serves 2

5g/⅛oz dried carrageen, a small sprig

600ml/1 pint/2½ cups milk of your choice

65g/2½oz dark (bittersweet) chocolate (minimum 70 per cent cocoa solids) broken into small chunks, plus extra for grating (optional)

a pinch of chilli powder (optional)

a pinch of sugar, if desired

50ml/2fl oz/¼ cup dark rum or whiskey

Cook's tip

To make this child friendly, use milk chocolate and omit the chilli powder and alcohol. It is extremely rich, however, so you may find it best to also double the volume of milk and serve it to more children.

Put the carrageen in a pan with the milk. Bring to the boil, then reduce the heat and simmer the mixture for 5–10 minutes, whisking occasionally.

Pour the infused milk through a strainer to remove any pieces of carrageen that haven't dissolved.

Return the milk to the pan and place over a low heat. Add the chocolate, stir until melted, then add the chilli powder and sugar, if using.

Pour the rum or whiskey into two mugs and pour the chocolate mixture on top. Grate over a little extra chocolate for an uber-decadent treat!

BLOODY MARY

Famous for its purported restorative qualities, this classic hair-of-the-dog is given a nutritious twist here with the addition of kelp-infused vodka. This unconventional steeping ingredient imparts a minerally flavour and saline depth to the alcohol that pairs very well with the acidic tomatoes and other umami ingredients.

Serves 1

50ml/2fl oz/¼ cup kelp-infused vodka (see Cook's tip opposite)

150ml/¼ pint/⅔ cup tomato juice

15ml/1 tbsp freshly squeezed lemon juice

a healthy pinch each of celery salt and ground black pepper

3 drops of Tabasco sauce

3 dashes of Worcestershire sauce

a drop of agave syrup or sugar syrup

ice

25ml/1½ tbsp dry sherry

a stick of celery, to garnish

a strip of dried kelp, to garnish (optional)

sumac or ground black pepper, to garnish

Put the kelp-infused vodka, tomato juice, lemon juice, celery salt and ground black pepper, Tabasco and Worcestershire sauces, and the syrup in a tall glass, top with ice and stir thoroughly to combine.

Taste and adjust the flavourings to suit your palate; add the Tabasco sauce a drop at at time.

Float the sherry on the top. By putting the sherry on top of the drink in this way, you'll be simultaneously hit by the aroma of the sherry along with the umami taste of the kelp on you first sip, and as you drink, the cocktail will develop and blend nicely. Garnish the glass with a stick of celery, a strip of kelp and a light dusting of sumac, if you have it – use ground black pepper if not.

KELP MARTINI

Whether you like them shaken or stirred, Martinis hit the sweet spot for many people, jolting the senses and getting the party started. Here, the marine flavour of the kelp-infused vodka is intensified by the distinctive flavour of the precious juice from a fresh oyster. Just close your eyes, have a sip and imagine you are by the sea…

Serves 1

50ml/2fl oz/¼ cup kelp-infused vodka (see Cook's tip)

10ml/2 tsp dry white vermouth

1 very fresh oyster

ice

a strip of kelp, to garnish (optional)

Combine the kelp-infused vodka and dry white vermouth in a mixing glass.

Carefully shuck the oyster (see page 171) and pour the liquor into the martini mixture, saving the oyster itself to eat with the cocktail.

Add ice to the Martini and stir thoroughly until it's ice cold. Strain into a chilled Martini glass or champagne saucer.

Variation
Instead of infusing the vodka with kelp you could try dulse, or have a play around with other types or combinations of seaweeds to see what works best for you.

Cook's tip
To make the kelp-infused vodka, simply add a long strand of fresh or dried kelp to a bottle of good-quality vodka and allow it to infuse for at least 8–10 hours.

APPLE, CUCUMBER, GINGER & SEAWEED JUICE

A doddle to blitz up in a blender, this soothing sea-green tonic is ideal for a hot day or when you feel you could do with a nutrient boost. Experiment with the proportions, adding as little or as much seaweed as you like, and try replacing the fresh root ginger with a few fresh mint leaves.

Serves 1

1 apple

½ cucumber

2.5cm/1in piece of fresh root ginger

a squeeze of lemon juice

10ml/2 tsp flaked sea greens or 15ml/1 tbsp fresh sea greens, snipped into small pieces

ice, for serving

Core the apple, then chop both it and the cucumber into chunks. Put these in a blender.

Peel the ginger and chop it into small pieces, then add to the blender together with the lemon juice and sea greens. Blend all ingredients together.

Put the ice cubes in a glass and pour over the juice.

TROPICAL SEA GREEN SMOOTHIE

This thick, zingy smoothie is lovely for breakfast or as a cooling snack on a hot afternoon, especially if you use frozen prepared mango as well as frozen banana. The sea greens really enhance the sweetness and tropical tang of the fruits, while the ginger provides a fragrant peppery lift. Delicious.

Serves 1

½ frozen banana

1cm/½in piece of fresh root ginger

½ ripe mango

10ml/2 tsp flaked sea greens or 15ml/1 tbsp fresh sea greens, snipped into small pieces

200ml/7fl oz/scant 1 cup cold water

Peel the banana and ginger, chop them into pieces and place them in a blender.

Slice off one 'cheek' of the mango, cut away the skin and roughly dice the flesh.

Add this to the blender with the sea greens and water and blitz until well blended.

Pour the smoothie into a glass and serve immediately.

NUTRITIONAL INFORMATION

The nutritional analysis given for each recipe is calculated per portion (i.e. serving or item), unless otherwise stated. If the recipe gives a range, such as Serves 4–6, then the nutritional analysis will be for the smaller portion size, i.e. 6 servings. The analysis does not include optional ingredients, such as salt added to taste.

p80 Seaweed Fish Stock (1 litre) Energy 80kcal/310kJ; Protein 1g; Carbohydrate 9.7g, of which sugars 1.1g; Fat 4g, of which saturates 1g; Cholesterol 0mg; Calcium 0mg; Fibre 0g; Sodium 0mg.

p81 Smoked Mackerel & Kelp Dashi Stock (500ml) Energy 40kcal/155kJ; Protein 0.5g; Carbohydrate 4.8g, of which sugars 0.5g; Fat 2g, of which saturates 0.5g; Cholesterol 0mg; Calcium 0mg; Fibre 0g; Sodium 0mg.

p83 Tomato Gazpacho with Crispy Sea Greens (serves 8) Energy 144kcal/603kJ; Protein 2.4g; Carbohydrate 9.6g, of which sugars 7.5g; Fat 11.1g, of which saturates 1.4g; Cholesterol 0mg; Calcium 44mg; Fibre 2.6g; Sodium 807mg.

p84 Jerusalem Artichoke & Dulse Soup (serves 6) Energy 102kcal/449kJ; Protein 2.5g; Carbohydrate 14.4g, of which sugars 3.9g; Fat 4.8g, of which saturates 0.7g; Cholesterol 0mg; Calcium 51mg; Fibre 7.2g; Sodium 17mg.

p86 Porcini & Sea Spaghetti Broth (Serves 4) Energy 87kcal/338kJ; Protein 1.1g; Carbohydrate 10.5g, of which sugars 1.1g; Fat 4.4g, of which saturates 1.1g; Cholesterol 0mg; Calcium 0mg; Fibre 0g; Sodium 0mg.

p87 Kale, Sea Greens & Coconut Soup (serves 2) Energy 150kcal/632kJ; Protein 8.5g; Carbohydrate 13.8g, of which sugars 10.8g; Fat 7.3g, of which saturates 5.4g; Cholesterol 0mg; Calcium 192mg; Fibre 12.1g; Sodium 361mg.

p89 All-Green Soup (serves 4) Energy 145kcal/603kJ; Protein 8.2g; Carbohydrate 12.1g, of which sugars 7.9g; Fat 7.3g, of which saturates 1.1g; Cholesterol 0mg; Calcium 183mg; Fibre 12.9g; Sodium 90mg.

p90 Butternut Squash Soup with Squash & Sea Salad Slaw (serves 8) Energy 129kcal/544kJ; Protein 2.2g; Carbohydrate 15.6g, of which sugars 8.5g; Fat 7g, of which saturates 3.5g; Cholesterol 16mg; Calcium 97mg; Fibre 4.5g; Sodium 63mg.

p93 Creamy Mushroom & Kelp Soup (serves 4) Energy 226kcal/938kJ; Protein 5g; Carbohydrate 12.3g, of which sugars 5.3g; Fat 17.8g, of which saturates 10.9g; Cholesterol 45mg; Calcium 194mg; Fibre 12g; Sodium 281mg.

p94 Smoked Mackerel & Spring Greens Ramen (serves 4) Energy 338kcal/1409kJ; Protein 16.6g; Carbohydrate 26.3g, of which sugars 3.1g; Fat 19.1g, of which saturates 4g; Cholesterol 110mg;

Calcium 107mg; Fibre 5.8g; Sodium 430mg.

p97 Cullen Skink with Sea Greens (serves 2) Energy 393kcal/1657kJ; Protein 36.6g; Carbohydrate 36.9g, of which sugars 17.8g; Fat 12g, of which saturates 7.1g; Cholesterol 120mg; Calcium 359mg; Fibre 6.3g; Sodium 1139mg.

p99 Pho Tai with Kelp (serves 6) Energy 512kcal/2141kJ; Protein 31.5g; Carbohydrate 69.7g, of which sugars 1.7g; Fat 10.7g, of which saturates 3.4g; Cholesterol 66mg; Calcium 16mg; Fibre 0g; Sodium 88mg.

p104 Seaweed Superspread (makes 1 jar) Energy 8kcal/33kJ; Protein 1.5g; Carbohydrate 0g, of which sugars 0g; Fat 0.2g, of which saturates 0g; Cholesterol 0mg; Calcium 72mg; Fibre 16.4g; Sodium 67mg.

p105 Dulse & Cheese Fondue (serves 6) Energy 683kcal/2832kJ; Protein 41.2g; Carbohydrate 1.4g, of which sugars 1.1g; Fat 56.4g, of which saturates 33.6g; Cholesterol 150mg; Calcium 1264mg; Fibre 1.8g; Sodium 1254mg.

p106 Sea Spaghetti-Stuffed Mushrooms Topped with Dulse Crust (serves 4) Energy 443kcal/1843kJ; Protein 19.1g; Carbohydrate 17g, of which sugars 2.5g; Fat 33.7g, of which saturates 14.8g; Cholesterol 66mg; Calcium 198mg; Fibre 8.7g; Sodium 426mg.

p109 Shrimp Ceviche with Sea Salad Popcorn (serves 4) Energy 521kcal/2172kJ; Protein 35.8g; Carbohydrate 28.3g, of which sugars 3.4g; Fat 30.1g, of which saturates 3.5g; Cholesterol 163mg; Calcium 450mg; Fibre 5.4g; Sodium 4863mg.

p110 Dulse & Seared Scallops (serves 2) Energy 484kcal/2031kJ; Protein 58.7g; Carbohydrate 8.7g, of which sugars 0.2g; Fat 24.2g, of which saturates 14.1g; Cholesterol 171mg; Calcium 145mg; Fibre 5.9g; Sodium 739mg.

p113 Deep-Fried Kelp-Wrapped Brie with Raspberry & Chilli Jam (serves 2) Energy 672kcal/2794kJ; Protein 28.6g; Carbohydrate 20.3g, of which sugars 20.3g; Fat 53.6g, of which saturates 25.4g; Cholesterol 116mg; Calcium 575mg; Fibre 22.9g; Sodium 1156mg.

p114 Poached Eggs & Smoked Salmon with Pepper Dulse & Sea Beets (serves 4) Energy 258kcal/1081kJ; Protein 23.8g; Carbohydrate 12.6g, of which sugars 0.9g; Fat 12.9g, of which saturates 4.4g; Cholesterol 257mg; Calcium 87mg; Fibre 3.6g; Sodium 1213mg.

p115 Pickled Kelp, Tomato & Melted Cheese Panini (serves 2) Energy 431kcal/1818kJ; Protein 19.8g; Carbohydrate 56.5g, of which sugars 4.3g; Fat 15.6g, of which saturates 8.8g; Cholesterol 36mg; Calcium 548mg; Fibre 11.4g; Sodium 1115mg.

p116 Mackerel Pâté with Sea Greens (serves 4) Energy 418kcal/1731kJ; Protein 11g; Carbohydrate 0.6g, of which sugars 0.6g; Fat 41.2g, of which saturates 19.4g; Cholesterol 122mg; Calcium 36mg; Fibre 2.2g; Sodium 409mg.

p119 Chickpea & Sea Salad Scotch Eggs (serves 4) Energy 443kcal/1861kJ; Protein 26.1g; Carbohydrate 42.7g, of which sugars 1.5g; Fat 19.5g, of which saturates 3.6g; Cholesterol 289mg; Calcium 143mg; Fibre 6.7g; Sodium 480mg.

p122 Lamb & Sea Spaghetti Dolmades (makes 25) Energy 34kcal/144kJ; Protein 2.9g; Carbohydrate 2.5g, of which sugars 0.7g; Fat 1.5g, of which saturates 0.7g; Cholesterol 8mg; Calcium 18mg; Fibre 1.5g; Sodium 21mg.

p124 Seaweed Crisps (serves 1) Energy 244kcal/1011kJ; Protein 6.5g; Carbohydrate 1.4g, of which sugars 1.3g; Fat 23.7g, of which saturates 1.7g; Cholesterol 0mg; Calcium 173mg; Fibre 10.1g; Sodium 122mg.

p127 Sea Spaghetti Bhajis (serves 4) Energy 202kcal/846kJ; Protein 12.6g; Carbohydrate 18.4g, of which sugars 3g; Fat 9.7g, of which saturates 1.4g; Cholesterol 0mg; Calcium 145mg; Fibre 3.4g; Sodium 70mg.

p131 Courgette & Dulse Fritters (makes 16) Energy 95kcal/400kJ; Protein 6.9g; Carbohydrate 12.8g, of which sugars 1.7g; Fat 1.9g, of which saturates 1.3g; Cholesterol 0mg; Calcium 26mg; Fibre 1.2g; Sodium 106mg.

p132 Seasalt Battered-Rock Salmon Goujons (serves 2) Energy 402kcal/1676kJ; Protein 26.2g; Carbohydrate 19g, of which sugars 0g; Fat 25g, of which saturates 2.6g; Cholesterol 0mg; Calcium 109mg; Fibre 1.1g; Sodium 260mg.

p136 Vegetable Seaweed Daal (serves 4) Energy 287kcal/1210kJ; Protein 18.2g; Carbohydrate 42.1g, of which sugars 10.6g; Fat 6.2g, of which saturates 0.9g; Cholesterol 17mg; Calcium 176mg; Fibre 15.2g; Sodium 163mg.

p139 Kelp Vegetable Chilli (serves 4) Energy 287kcal/1215kJ; Protein 11.7g; Carbohydrate

55g, of which sugars 24.7g; Fat 4g, of which saturates 0.7g; Cholesterol 0mg; Calcium 161mg; Fibre 17.2g; Sodium 697mg.

p141 Beetroot, Mushroom & Dulse Burgers (makes 10) Energy 149kcal/626kJ; Protein 4.8g; Carbohydrate 17.6g, of which sugars 3.8g; Fat 7.1g, of which saturates 1g; Cholesterol 46mg; Calcium 34mg; Fibre 3g; Sodium 52mg.

p144 Sea Aloo (serves 4) Energy 190kcal/798kJ; Protein 6g; Carbohydrate 28.2g, of which sugars 8.2g; Fat 6.7g, of which saturates 0.9g; Cholesterol 41mg; Calcium 130mg; Fibre 7.5g; Sodium 122mg.

p146 Sea Salad Moussaka (serves 4) Energy 654kcal/2715kJ; Protein 38.3g; Carbohydrate 11.6g, of which sugars 8.1g; Fat 50.8g, of which saturates 21.1g; Cholesterol 196mg; Calcium 467mg; Fibre 25.2g; Sodium 1258mg.

p149 Seaweed Lax Pudden (serves 4) Energy 540kcal/2255kJ; Protein 27.2g; Carbohydrate 31.3g, of which sugars 6.3g; Fat 34.7g, of which saturates 16.2g; Cholesterol 374mg; Calcium 185mg; Fibre 4.6g; Sodium 205mg.

p152 Sea Salad & Broccoli Quiche (serves 8) Energy 350kcal/1458kJ; Protein 11.6g; Carbohydrate 28.4g, of which sugars 3.8g; Fat 21.8g, of which saturates 11.8g; Cholesterol 132mg; Calcium 193mg; Fibre 3.5g; Sodium 221mg.

p155 Dairy-Free Seaweed & Vegetable Quiche (serves 6) Energy 354kcal/1473kJ; Protein 10.7g; Carbohydrate 28.6g, of which sugars 4.7g; Fat 22.6g, of which saturates 7.3g; Cholesterol 130mg; Calcium 128mg; Fibre 3.2g; Sodium 299mg.

p156 Leek, Mushroom & Dulse Omelette (serves 2) Energy 386kcal/1602kJ; Protein 23.8g; Carbohydrate 4.4g, of which sugars 2.4g; Fat 30.4g, of which saturates 12.8g; Cholesterol 501mg; Calcium 135mg; Fibre 3.6g; Sodium 367mg.

p159 Sea Paneer or Tofu (serves 4) Energy 141kcal/587kJ; Protein 8.1g; Carbohydrate 7g, of which sugars 4g; Fat 9.3g, of which saturates 1.3g; Cholesterol 0mg; Calcium 473mg; Fibre 8.7g; Sodium 263mg.

p160 Marinated Fish & Kelp Curry (serves 4) Energy 182kcal/763kJ; Protein 25.2g; Carbohydrate 8.5g, of which sugars 6.5g; Fat 5.5g, of which saturates 0.5g; Cholesterol 58mg; Calcium 73mg; Fibre 4.1g; Sodium 276mg.

p162 Thai Fish & Seaweed Pie (serve 6) Energy 217kcal/920kJ; Protein 20.2g; Carbohydrate 23.4g, of which sugars 9.6g; Fat 5.5g, of which saturates 3g; Cholesterol 68mg; Calcium 120mg; Fibre 6.7g; Sodium 822mg.

p165 Fish Seaweed Paella (serves 4) Energy 884kcal/3695kJ; Protein 77.7g; Carbohydrate 98.1g, of which sugars 3.3g; Fat 17.2g, of which

saturates 2.6g; Cholesterol 128mg; Calcium 111mg; Fibre 2.8g; Sodium 445mg.

p166 Hake & Kelp Saltimbocca (serves 4) Energy 127kcal/534kJ; Protein 23.4g; Carbohydrate 0g, of which sugars 0g; Fat 3.7g, of which saturates 0.6g; Cholesterol 29mg; Calcium 130mg; Fibre 9.8g; Sodium 354mg.

p168 Sea Spaghetti 'Tagliatelle' with Crab (serves 2) Energy 507kcal/2115kJ; Protein 64.7g; Carbohydrate 9.5g, of which sugars 8.6g; Fat 23.4g, of which saturates 3.2g; Cholesterol 216mg; Calcium 98mg; Fibre 10.7g; Sodium 1349mg.

p171 Baked Oyster Gratin (serves 4) Energy 543kcal/2285kJ; Protein 48.5g; Carbohydrate 43.1g, of which sugars 2.4g; Fat 20.8g, of which saturates 6.5g; Cholesterol 208mg; Calcium 619mg; Fibre 4.5g; Sodium 2248mg.

p173 Sea Greens Tempura Cuttlefish (serves 4) Energy 509kcal/2151kJ; Protein 34.8g; Carbohydrate 73.1g, of which sugars 1.3g; Fat 10.6g, of which saturates 1.5g; Cholesterol 165mg; Calcium 380mg; Fibre 8.2g; Sodium 842mg.

p181 Mackerel, Horseradish and Sea Greens Pasty (makes 4) Energy 1103kcal/4600kJ; Protein 22.6g; Carbohydrate 97.9g, of which sugars 4.6g; Fat 71.7g, of which saturates 41.1g; Cholesterol 204mg; Calcium 218mg; Fibre 8g; Sodium 561mg.

p181 Liver, Dulse and Mushroom Pasty (makes 4) Energy 1029kcal/4294kJ; Protein 21.1g; Carbohydrate 96.9g, of which sugars 4.8g; Fat 64.6g, of which saturates 39.7g; Cholesterol 270mg; Calcium 196mg; Fibre 7.5g; Sodium 514mg.

p182 Mushroom, Capers and Sea Spaghetti Pasty (makes 4) Energy 1018kcal/4244kJ; Protein 13.7g; Carbohydrate 97g, of which sugars 4.8g; Fat 66.6g, of which saturates 41.3g; Cholesterol 180mg; Calcium 201mg; Fibre 8.4g; Sodium 517mg.

p182 Pork, Apple and Dulse Pasty (makes 4) Energy 1055kcal/4402kJ; Protein 21.3g; Carbohydrate 102.8g, of which sugars 10.6g; Fat 64.9g, of which saturates 39.9g; Cholesterol 196mg; Calcium 198mg; Fibre 8.5g; Sodium 508mg.

p183 Stilton, Walnut and Sea Spaghetti Pasty (serves 4) Energy 1312kcal/5461kJ; Protein 25.8g; Carbohydrate 97.7g, of which sugars 5.4g; Fat 93.6g, of which saturates 49.9g; Cholesterol 208mg; Calcium 345mg; Fibre 9.2g; Sodium 790mg.

p183 Cheese, Onion and Sea Salad Pasty (makes 4) Energy 1311kcal/5460kJ; Protein 32.7g; Carbohydrate 99.5g, of which sugars 7.3g; Fat 89.7g, of which saturates 55.6g; Cholesterol 245mg; Calcium 780mg; Fibre 9.3g; Sodium 1043mg.

p185 Chicken, Mushroom & Sea Spaghetti Pie (serves 6) Energy 207kcal/870kJ; Protein 23.6g; Carbohydrate 12.1g, of which sugars 4.2g; Fat 7.5g, of which saturates 2.1g; Cholesterol 65mg; Calcium 82mg; Fibre 3.2g; Sodium 177mg.

p186 Sea Spaghetti, Beef & Guinness Pie (serves 6) Energy 412kcal/1726kJ; Protein 38.7g; Carbohydrate 21.6g, of which sugars 3.4g; Fat 17.8g, of which saturates 6.4g; Cholesterol 125mg; Calcium 163mg; Fibre 4.2g; Sodium 593mg.

p189 Kelp Lasagne Two Ways (serves 6) Energy 513kcal/2146kJ; Protein 20.8g; Carbohydrate 45.3g, of which sugars 16.1g; Fat 28.9g, of which saturates 15.9g; Cholesterol 78mg; Calcium 352mg; Fibre 8.8g; Sodium 403mg.

p195 Sea Spaghetti West-Country Salad (serves 4) Energy 362kcal/1506kJ; Protein 22.7g; Carbohydrate 8.3g, of which sugars 0.8g; Fat 26.7g, of which saturates 14.2g; Cholesterol 301mg; Calcium 421mg; Fibre 2.9g; Sodium 489mg.

p199 Quinoa, Sea Salad, Grilled Halloumi & Pomegranate Salad (serves 4) Energy 314kcal/1321kJ; Protein 16.8g; Carbohydrate 33.8g, of which sugars 9g; Fat 13.4g, of which saturates 4.5g; Cholesterol 15mg; Calcium 201mg; Fibre 11.2g; Sodium 249mg.

p200 Thai Crab, Mango & Sea Salad (serves 2) Energy 637kcal/2666kJ; Protein 59.2g; Carbohydrate 55.7g, of which sugars 14.6g; Fat 20g, of which saturates 2.7g; Cholesterol 180mg; Calcium 103mg; Fibre 12.9g; Sodium 1176mg.

p203 Tuna, Bean & Sea Salad (serves 4) Energy 245kcal/1037kJ; Protein 28.7g; Carbohydrate 24.1g, of which sugars 6.7g; Fat 4.5g, of which saturates 0.8g; Cholesterol 38mg; Calcium 103mg; Fibre 14.2g; Sodium 803mg.

p204 Cauliflower, Mushroom, Dulse & Tarragon 'Rice' (serves 4) Energy 101kcal/417kJ; Protein 5.3g; Carbohydrate 3.5g, of which sugars 2.9g; Fat 7.4g, of which saturates 4.2g; Cholesterol 16mg; Calcium 37mg; Fibre 4.6g; Sodium 77mg.

p207 Spicy Beetroot, Sea Salad & Sesame Salad (serves 4) Energy 112kcal/467kJ; Protein 6.1g; Carbohydrate 5.8g, of which sugars 5.3g; Fat 7.3g, of which saturates 1.2g; Cholesterol 0mg; Calcium 114mg; Fibre 9.4g; Sodium 140mg.

p208 Potato Salad (serves 4) Energy 199kcal/ 836kJ; Protein 6.3g; Carbohydrate 21.7g, of which sugars 3.2g; Fat 10.3g, of which saturates 1.7g; Cholesterol 57mg; Calcium 86mg; Fibre 8.6g; Sodium 148mg.

p210 Coleslaw with Sea Salad (serves 4) Energy 255kcal/1056kJ; Protein 7.7g; Carbohydrate 10.9g, of which sugars 10.4g; Fat 20.4g, of which saturates 3.2g; Cholesterol 31mg; Calcium 150mg; Fibre 15.1g; Sodium 222mg.

p211 Boiled Kelp (one portion 100g uncooked

weight) Energy 43kcal/180kJ; Protein 7.1g; Carbohydrate 0g, of which sugars 0g; Fat 1.6g, of which saturates 0.5g; Cholesterol 0mg; Calcium 900mg; Fibre 78.3g; Sodium 1830mg.

p211 Steamed Sea Spaghetti with Toasted Sesame Seeds and Soy Sauce (per 100g seaweed uncooked weight) Energy 264kcal/1097kJ; Protein 15.5g; Carbohydrate 1g, of which sugars 0.9g; Fat 22.1g, of which saturates 3.5g; Cholesterol 0mg; Calcium 763mg; Fibre 64.4g; Sodium 4006mg.

p212 Creamy Avocado and Dulse Pesto (serves 6) Energy 280kcal/1156kJ; Protein 7.3g; Carbohydrate 1.4g, of which sugars 0.6g; Fat 27.2g, of which saturates 3.8g; Cholesterol 0mg; Calcium 91mg; Fibre 9.4g; Sodium 102mg.

p212 Kelp Pesto (serves 6) Energy 175kcal/721kJ; Protein 4.4g; Carbohydrate 1g, of which sugars 0.4g; Fat 17.1g, of which saturates 3g; Cholesterol 6mg; Calcium 156mg; Fibre 5.4g; Sodium 174mg.

p215 Sea Salad Hummus (serves 6) Energy 134kcal/558kJ; Protein 5.5g; Carbohydrate 7g, of which sugars 0.2g; Fat 9.5g, of which saturates 1.3g; Cholesterol 0mg; Calcium 47mg; Fibre 6.3g; Sodium 148mg.

p216 Seaweed Raita/Tzatziki (serves 6) Energy 37kcal/155kJ; Protein 4.1g; Carbohydrate 4g, of which sugars 4g; Fat 0.6g, of which saturates 0.4g; Cholesterol 1mg; Calcium 106mg; Fibre 3.1g; Sodium 72mg.

p217 Spicy Ginger & Kelp Soy (makes 200ml) Energy 112kcal/472kJ; Protein 9g; Carbohydrate 18.5g, of which sugars 16.7g; Fat 0.6g, of which saturates 0.1g; Cholesterol 0mg; Calcium 312mg; Fibre 23.5g; Sodium 14795mg.

p218 Caper, Pepper Dulse & Horseradish Sauce (serves 6) Energy 26kcal/108kJ; Protein 1.8g; Carbohydrate 3.6g, of which sugars 3.4g; Fat 0.6g, of which saturates 0.3g; Cholesterol 1mg; Calcium 57mg; Fibre 0.2g; Sodium 44mg.

p219 Seaweed Salad Dressing (makes 175ml) Energy 751kcal/3092kJ; Protein 3.9g; Carbohydrate 4.4g, of which sugars 4.4g; Fat 78.1g, of which saturates 11.1g; Cholesterol 0mg; Calcium 58mg; Fibre 6.6g; Sodium 243mg.

p222 Baked Apples with a Sea Greens & Rum Caramel Sauce (serves 4) Energy 993kcal/4158kJ; Protein 3.9g; Carbohydrate 125.2g, of which sugars 125.2g; Fat 54.6g, of which saturates 34.2g; Cholesterol 140mg; Calcium 97mg; Fibre 5.8g; Sodium 288mg.

p225 Blackberry, Apple & Dulse Crumble (serves 6) Energy 281kcal/1182kJ; Protein 4.1g; Carbohydrate 42.9g, of which sugars 21g; Fat 11.6g, of which saturates 6.6g; Cholesterol 27mg; Calcium 79mg; Fibre 5.6g; Sodium 90mg.

p226 Dairy-Free Chocolate Mousse (serves 4) Energy 278kcal/1158kJ; Protein 4.6g;

Carbohydrate 20.9g, of which sugars 17.8g; Fat 20.2g, of which saturates 10.3g; Cholesterol 0mg; Calcium 26mg; Fibre 4.8g; Sodium 112mg.

p227 Carrageen Vanilla Jelly (serves 4) Energy 124kcal/523kJ; Protein 7.1g; Carbohydrate 14.9g, of which sugars 14.9g; Fat 4.4g, of which saturates 2.5g; Cholesterol 64mg; Calcium 222mg; Fibre 2.1g; Sodium 105mg.

p231 Chai Seaweed Panna Cotta with Mango (serves 6) Energy 610kcal/2528kJ; Protein 6.2g; Carbohydrate 31.3g, of which sugars 31.1g; Fat 52g, of which saturates 32.5g; Cholesterol 131mg; Calcium 183mg; Fibre 0.9g; Sodium 88mg.

p232 Tangy Raspberry Moss Pots (serves 6) Energy 76kcal/321kJ; Protein 2.9g; Carbohydrate 11.6g, of which sugars 11.6g; Fat 2.3g, of which saturates 0.7g; Cholesterol 77mg; Calcium 21mg; Fibre 0.8g; Sodium 29mg.

p235 Raw Cheesecake (serves 10) Energy 394kcal/1631kJ; Protein 9.4g; Carbohydrate 10.3g, of which sugars 7.4g; Fat 35.3g, of which saturates 7.1g; Cholesterol 0mg; Calcium 57mg; Fibre 5.1g; Sodium 31mg.

p237 Chocolate Tart with Dulse Caramel (serves 8) Energy 567kcal/2355kJ; Protein 6.8g; Carbohydrate 37.5g, of which sugars 28.5g; Fat 44.4g, of which saturates 22.4g; Cholesterol 175mg; Calcium 69mg; Fibre 2.1g; Sodium 211mg.

p241 Pepper Truffles (makes 40) Energy 105kcal/435kJ; Protein 0.9g; Carbohydrate 6.6g, of which sugars 6.4g; Fat 8.5g, of which saturates 5g; Cholesterol 14mg; Calcium 9mg; Fibre 0.5g; Sodium 9mg.

p245 Rhubarb, Date & Nori Slices (makes 16) Energy 237kcal/999kJ; Protein 3.8g; Carbohydrate 35.9g, of which sugars 24.4g; Fat 9.7g, of which saturates 5.1g; Cholesterol 49mg; Calcium 43mg; Fibre 2.7g; Sodium 80mg.

p247 Chilli, Walnut & Orange Gluten-Free Chocolate Brownies (makes 16) Energy 321kcal/1344kJ; Protein 4.8g; Carbohydrate 25.2g, of which sugars 24.4g; Fat 22.9g, of which saturates 11.4g; Cholesterol 92mg; Calcium 36mg; Fibre 1.3g; Sodium 68mg.

p250 Carrot, Sea Spaghetti & Pumpkin Seed Cake (serves 8) Energy 652kcal/2728kJ; Protein 11.4g; Carbohydrate 72.9g, of which sugars 50.1g; Fat 36.9g, of which saturates 12.7g; Cholesterol 145mg; Calcium 195mg; Fibre 4.1g; Sodium 255mg.

p252 Sea Baklava (makes 15) Energy 331kcal/1384kJ; Protein 3.1g; Carbohydrate 26.7g, of which sugars 26.5g; Fat 24.2g, of which saturates 8.2g; Cholesterol 29mg; Calcium 33mg; Fibre 0.9g; Sodium 3mg.

p254 Sea Spaghetti & Nut Banana Bread (makes 1 loaf) Energy 1885kcal/7930kJ; Protein 28.4g; Carbohydrate 300.1g, of which sugars 159.8g;

Fat 71.5g, of which saturates 41.6g; Cholesterol 391mg; Calcium 337mg; Fibre 11.6g; Sodium 551mg.

p257 Cheese & Dulse Scones (makes 20) Energy 110kcal/465kJ; Protein 3.1g; Carbohydrate 18.1g, of which sugars 0.9g; Fat 3.3g, of which saturates 2g; Cholesterol 9mg; Calcium 62mg; Fibre 0.9g; Sodium 38mg.

p260 Sea Salad Oat Cakes (makes 20) Energy 110kcal/462kJ; Protein 2.6g; Carbohydrate 15.5g, of which sugars 0g; Fat 4.6g, of which saturates 0.4g; Cholesterol 0mg; Calcium 12mg; Fibre 1.9g; Sodium 56mg.

p263 Sea Greens Soda Bread (makes 1 loaf) Energy 1568kcal/6666kJ; Protein 60.8g; Carbohydrate 330.1g, of which sugars 23.2g; Fat 9.6g, of which saturates 2g; Cholesterol 6mg; Calcium 736mg; Fibre 38.3g; Sodium 2146mg.

p264 Gluten-Free Dulse Flatbread (makes 6) Energy 72kcal/306kJ; Protein 4.3g; Carbohydrate 10.8g, of which sugars 0.6g; Fat 1.7g, of which saturates 0.2g; Cholesterol 0mg; Calcium 39mg; Fibre 3.1g; Sodium 9mg.

p267 Sea Salad & Pepper Dulse Bread Rolls (makes 12) Energy 148kcal/629kJ; Protein 3.8g; Carbohydrate 30.5g, of which sugars 1.9g; Fat 2.8g, of which saturates 1.2g; Cholesterol 4mg; Calcium 73mg; Fibre 1.6g; Sodium 14mg.

p268 Focaccia with Flaked Sea Greens & Rosemary (makes 1) Energy 1575kcal/6694kJ; Protein 45.4g; Carbohydrate 349.6g, of which sugars 6.8g; Fat 9g, of which saturates 1.4g; Cholesterol 0mg; Calcium 674mg; Fibre 24.5g; Sodium 4022mg.

p272 Boozy Chilli & Carrageen Hot Chocolate (serves 2) Energy 360kcal/1507kJ; Protein 11.6g; Carbohydrate 35.4g, of which sugars 35.1g; Fat 13.9g, of which saturates 8.8g; Cholesterol 23mg; Calcium 343mg; Fibre 1.5g; Sodium 154mg.

p274 Bloody Mary (makes 1) Energy 164kcal/687kJ; Protein 1.3g; Carbohydrate 5.6g, of which sugars 5.6g; Fat 0g, of which saturates 0g; Cholesterol 0mg; Calcium 26mg; Fibre 1.2g; Sodium 408mg.

p275 Kelp Martini (serves 1) Energy 122kcal/505kJ; Protein 0g; Carbohydrate 0.3g, of which sugars 0.3g; Fat 0g, of which saturates 0g; Cholesterol 0mg; Calcium 1mg; Fibre 0g; Sodium 1mg.

p276 Apple, Cucumber, Ginger & Seaweed Juice (serves 1) Energy 60kcal/251kJ; Protein 4.4g; Carbohydrate 10.2g, of which sugars 10g; Fat 0.4g, of which saturates 0g; Cholesterol 0mg; Calcium 73mg; Fibre 8.7g; Sodium 86mg.

p277 Tropical Sea Green Smoothie (serves 1) Energy 104kcal/443kJ; Protein 4.2g; Carbohydrate 22.2g, of which sugars 20.8g; Fat 0.4g, of which saturates 0.2g; Cholesterol 0mg; Calcium 55mg; Fibre 9.3g; Sodium 81mg.

INDEX

THE CORNISH SEAWEED COMPANY

Revered for its crystal-clear waters and southern swell rolling away beneath the tin mines, Cornwall has a history of doing things differently. The Cornish Seaweed Company – a small sustainable company set up by two friends, Caroline Warwick-Evans and Tim van Berkel, in 2012 – is no different, and is now one of the UK's leaders in the industry of harvesting edible seaweed, at a time when the abundant algae are becoming increasingly popular in households across the nation.

Back in 2012, Caro and Tim were doing ad-hoc work, such as waiting tables and cleaning boats, living in caravans, and making the most of the Cornish seas by surfing whenever possible. With backgrounds in renewable energy and nature conservation, the friends would discuss what they could do to make the most of their skills, and create meaningful work in Cornwall.

Early one morning, as Caro was strapping up her wetsuit she heard somebody speaking on the BBC Radio 4 programme *Farming Today* about the seaweed industry in Ireland. Inspired, she and Tim travelled to Ireland to learn the skills of hand harvesting, processing and drying edible seaweeds. On their return, they embarked on the often difficult task of starting the first seaweed company based in England, working in collaboration with Natural England, the Crown Estate and the Food Standards Agency.

In the beginning, Tim and Caro dreamed of creating employment and volunteer opportunities which would help get seaweed into as many homes as possible in England . These dreams have come to fruition and the company has provided employment in the county for a dozen people as well as volunteer opportunities by teaming up with local organisations helping to get people back into employment.

As a business they are still growing. Since setting up they have come from building drying units using reclaimed wood, and living in caravans and packing at night-times in a friend's bakery, to running a successful business selling their products both nationally and internationally. They have also won the accolade of Cornish Business of the Year at the Hub Awards and Cornwall's Sustainability Award where they won Best Contribution to a Sustainable Economy. They have been featured on television and in other media, each article or programme helping to raise the awareness about seaweed and what a wonderful, sustainable resource it is on our seashores.

With its position as a foodie mecca, Cornwall is blessed with world-class Michelin-starred restaurants running the length and breadth of its shoreline. Be it the eateries of Rick Stein, Nathan Outlaw or Jamie Oliver, or the soup kitchens and schools of West Penwith, any chef worth their (sea) salt in Cornwall now uses seaweed as part of their menus. Drawing upon this clientele, The Cornish Seaweed Company worked with several chefs and seaweed home cooks in order to compile the recipes contained in this book, as a means of demonstrating the flexibility, variety and accessibility of seaweed as a flavouring, ingredient and vegetable. Abundant, sustainable and nutritious, this ancient ingredient is now being acclaimed as the food of the future.

For more information see our website
www.cornishseaweed.co.uk

ACKNOWLEDGEMENTS

This edition is published by Lorenz Books
an imprint of Anness Publishing Ltd
info@anness.com
www.lorenzbooks.com
wwwannesspublishing.com

A CIP catalogue record for this book is available from the British Library.

Publisher: Joanna Lorenz
Editor: Lucy Doncaster
Editorial assistant: Sarah Lumby
Special photography: David Griffen
Food for photography: James Porter
Additional photography: Tom Holmes
Designer: Adelle Mahoney
Nutritional consultant: Clare Emery
Seaweed consultants: Dr Gavin Hardy, Prof. M.D. Guiry (AlgaeBase, NUI, Galway)

PUBLISHER'S NOTE

Although the advice and information in this book are believed to be accurate and true at the time of going to press, neither the author nor the publisher can accept any legal responsibility or liability for any errors or omissions that may have been made nor for any inaccuracies nor for any loss, harm or injury that comes about from following instructions or advice in this book.

PICTURE CREDITS

The publisher would like to thank the following for the use of their pictures in the book (l= left, r=right, t=top, b=bottom, c=centre): The Cornish Seaweed Company: p2, p7, p15, p20, p23, p30, p38, p67l, p67br, p69cl, p122, p128, p249, p267, p287; Shutterstock.com: p9, p22, p24, p33, p61br, p174-5; iStockphoto.com: p10, p17, p25, p27, p51tl, p52b, p53b, p53t, p54r, p54l, p55, p90, p101; Alamy: p11, p32, p42, p44, p51tr, p52t, p75, p151; Nicki Dowey: p226; M.D. Guiry (AlgaeBase): p46 both images in box, p49, p51b. All other photographs David Griffen and Tom Holmes © Anness Publishing Ltd.

AUTHORS' NOTE

A project that has now spanned three years and seen a huge number of delicious dishes created, tweaked and devoured, photographed and edited would not have been able to come to fruition without the determined, dedicated and passionate individuals we were lucky enough to work with.

Special thanks to Daisy Parsons and Laura Barnes who together devised, tried and tested a huge number of recipes that have made it into this book. Their creativity and hard work have ensured we have a wonderful and diverse selection of recipes forming the backbone of this book. We would also like to say a huge thank you to all our friends and chefs who have helped create such fantastic recipes as well as Grace Chinn, Jolie Blanchard and Ben Pryor. A big thank you also goes out to Joe, who has been a great taster of recipes and solid support through this time, which has seen a lot of changes occur!

Visually the finished book would not be what it is without the great imagery gathered over the last few years from several friends who we owe a big thank you to: Danny and Jonny at Kingdom and Sparrow who have spent many a day photographing us to capture the essence of The Cornish Seaweed Company since we set out in 2012, and who have also offered a helping hand to tweak the final design of the book. A recent graduate in Photography from Falmouth Art School, Tom Holmes has also spent many an hour with us with a camera slung over his shoulder. And thanks to Emli Bendixen for some amazing half-under half-above water harvest shots.

Head chef Jamie Porter teamed up with Food Photographer of The Year David Griffen to create and document our beautiful recipes.

After three years of work with our dedicated and patient publisher Joanna, we have finally finished this book. This would not have been possible without her experience, understanding and dedication and we are happy to have worked with her.

COOK'S NOTES

Bracketed terms are intended for American readers.

For all recipes, quantities are given in both metric and imperial measures and, where appropriate, in standard cups and spoons. Follow one set of measures, but not a mixture, because they are not interchangeable. Standard spoon and cup measures are level. 1 tsp = 5ml, 1 tbsp = 15ml, 1 cup = 250ml/8fl oz.

Australian standard tablespoons are 20ml. Australian readers should use 3 tsp in place of 1 tbsp for measuring small quantities.

American pints are 16fl oz/2 cups. American readers should use 20fl oz/2.5 cups in place of 1 pint when measuring liquids.

Since ovens vary, you should check with your manufacturer's instruction book for guidance.

Medium (US large) eggs are used unless otherwise stated.

IMPORTANT CAUTIONS

Any foraging for seaweeds should be undertaken responsibly, from permitted sites and harvesting from clean water, please see page 60 for more details. Our commercial seaweeds are tested in laboratories for heavy metals and microbiological activity. This book is a guide to cooking with seaweeds and is not intended as a detailed identification or foraging handbook.

Certain seaweeds are naturally rich in iodine, and excess intake may affect thyroid function; the maximum recommended daily intake is 5g. See page 18 for more details. There are some concerns about carageenan, see page 36 for more details.

Due care should be taken with the type and amount of seaweeds ingested and appropriate advice should be sought from a medical professional if you have a particular health or dietary condition, are cooking for the young or elderly, or for anyone who is pregnant.